Biography

Pro
_of I_
_of I_
_to Y_
Rea

615 Griswold Street
Detroit, Mi

ISSN 1058-2347 • ISBN 0-7808-0814-2

This book is printed on acid-free paper meeting the ANSI Z39.48 Standard. The infinity symbol that appears above indicates that the paper in this book meets that standard.

Printed in the United States

Contents

Preface

Biography Today is a magazine designed and written for the young reader—ages 9 and above—and covers individuals that librarians and teachers tell us that young people want to know about most: entertainers, athletes, writers, illustrators, cartoonists, and political leaders.

The Plan of the Work

The publication was especially created to appeal to young readers in a format they can enjoy reading and readily understand. Each issue contains approximately 10 sketches arranged alphabetically. Each entry provides at least one picture of the individual profiled, and bold-faced rubrics lead the reader to information on birth, youth, early memories, education, first jobs, marriage and family, career highlights, memorable experiences, hobbies, and honors and awards. Each of the entries ends with a list of easily accessible sources designed to lead the student to further reading on the individual and a current address. Retrospective entries are also included, written to provide a perspective on the individual's entire career.

Biographies are prepared by Omnigraphics editors after extensive research, utilizing the most current materials available. Those sources that are generally available to students appear in the list of further reading at the end of the sketch.

Indexes

Cumulative indexes are an important component of *Biography Today*. Each issue of the *Biography Today* General Series includes a Cumulative Names Index, which comprises all individuals profiled in *Biography Today* since the series began in 1992. In addition, we compile three other indexes: the Cumulative General Index, Places of Birth Index, and Birthday Index. See our web site, www.biographytoday.com, for these three indexes, along with the Names Index. All *Biography Today* indexes are cumulative, including all individuals profiled in both the General Series and the Subject Series.

Our Advisors

This series was reviewed by an Advisory Board comprised of librarians, children's literature specialists, and reading instructors to ensure that the concept of this publication — to provide a readable and accessible biographical magazine for young readers — was on target. They evaluated the title as it developed, and their suggestions have proved invaluable. Any errors, however, are ours alone. We'd like to list the Advisory Board members, and to thank them for their efforts.

Gail Beaver
Adjunct Lecturer
University of Michigan
Ann Arbor, MI

Cindy Cares
Youth Services Librarian
Southfield Public Library
Southfield, MI

Carol A. Doll
School of Information Science and Policy
University of Albany, SUNY
Albany, NY

Kathleen Hayes-Parvin
Language Arts Teacher
Birney Middle School
Southfield, MI

Karen Imarisio
Assistant Head of Adult Services
Bloomfield Twp. Public Library
Bloomfield Hills, MI

Rosemary Orlando
Director
St. Clair Shores Public Library
St. Clair Shores, MI

Our Advisory Board stressed to us that we should not shy away from controversial or unconventional people in our profiles, and we have tried to follow their advice. The Advisory Board also mentioned that the sketches might be useful in reluctant reader and adult literacy programs, and we would value any comments librarians might have about the suitability of our magazine for those purposes.

Your Comments Are Welcome

Our goal is to be accurate and up-to-date, to give young readers information they can learn from and enjoy. Now we want to know what you think. Take a look at this issue of *Biography Today,* on approval. Write or call me with your comments. We want to provide an excellent source of biographical information for young people. Let us know how you think we're doing.

Cherie Abbey
Managing Editor, *Biography Today*
Omnigraphics, Inc.
615 Griswold Street
Detroit, MI 48226

editor@biographytoday.com
www.biographytoday.com

Congratulations!

Congratulations to the following individuals and libraries, who are receiving a free copy of *Biography Today*, Vol. 15, No. 3 for suggesting people who appear in this issue:

Renee Laune, New Haven, MO

Sarah Puckett, Northville, MI

Mary Beth Rapai, Frenchtown Township, MI

Rick Rill, Crystal Lake South High School Library, Crystal Lake, IL

Ashley Squires, Charlotte, NC

Theresa Velez-Balay, Rio Linda Junior High School Library, Rio Linda, CA

Joyce Word, Watkins Middle School Library, Houston, TX

Bono 1960-

Irish Musician and Political Activist
Lead Singer and Songwriter for the Rock Group U2
Influential Advocate for Africa, AIDS Victims, and
Debt Relief for Third-World Countries

BIRTH

Bono was born Paul David Hewson on May 10, 1960, in Dublin, Ireland. His father, Robert Hewson, was a postal worker, and his mother, Iris (Rankin) Hewson, was a secretary in a dairy. His only brother, Norman, is seven years older. Norman runs a café in Dublin and has been involved in business ventures with Bono.

YOUTH

Bono was the child of a "mixed marriage": his mother was a Protestant and his father was a Roman Catholic in a strongly Catholic country. When Bono was a boy, children of so-called "mixed marriages" in Ireland were expected to be brought up as Catholics. But his mother raised her sons as Protestants. On Sundays, his father would drop the two boys and their mother off at a Protestant chapel, then wait outside during the service.

This small divide in his family reflected the serious and brutal split that existed in nearby Northern Ireland. The United Kingdom (UK) is made up of four countries: Northern Ireland, plus England, Scotland, and Wales (these three together make up Great Britain). Bono grew up in the Republic of Ireland (usually called just Ireland), which is a separate country. Fierce religious divisions have affected this region. The predominant religion in the United Kingdom is Protestantism, while the predominant religion in Ireland is Catholicism. Northern Ireland included both of these groups: Protestants were the majority and were aligned with the ruling United Kingdom, while Catholics were the minority and wanted the nation to break off from the UK to become part of the independent Republic of Ireland to the south. Brutal violence between the two groups, known as "the troubles," became a regular occurrence through much of the later 20th century.

"The death of my mother really affected my confidence. I would go back to my house after school, but it wasn't a home. . . . I felt abandoned, afraid. I guess fear converts to anger pretty quickly. It's still with me."

Throughout his childhood, Bono was aware of the violence that played out almost daily in the struggle between the two factions in Northern Ireland. Although he is an avowed Christian, Bono came away with distaste for organized religion. As he explained to radio host Larry King: "I learned that religion is often the enemy of God. . . . Religion is the artifice—you know, the building—after God has left it."

Bono has very little memory of his childhood. "The little pieces that I can put back together are, if not violent, then aggressive," he said. His relationship with his father was difficult, because his father was often critical and distant. His relationship with his mother was warmer, but she died suddenly after suffering a stroke at her own father's funeral. Bono was only 14 at the time, and the loss was difficult for him: "The death of my mother really affected my confidence. I would go back to my house after school, but it wasn't a home. . . . I felt abandoned, afraid. I guess fear converts to anger pretty quickly. It's still with me."

Bono began to channel his emotions into creative activities, including painting, acting, and ultimately music. In spite of the difficulties at home, music had always filled the Hewson household—anything from Frank Sinatra to classical to opera, which Bono's father loved. "His dad had an incredible voice," a childhood friend said. Bono's older brother taught him to play the guitar and exposed him to the Beatles and other rock groups. John Lennon, with his superb song writing and idealistic vision of world peace, was a major influence on Bono. "I was 13, I suppose, and I became enthralled with his dream," he said. The English new-wave group The Clash was another influence. After he heard them, "a band was what he wanted to do," said his friend Bob Geldof, the singer and leader of the Boomtown Rats, an Irish rock band.

EDUCATION

Bono attended Glasnevin National Primary School in Dublin, where he was a successful and popular student. At age 11, he moved to the next stage of Irish education at a Catholic all-boys' school called St. Patrick's. But things changed there. He lost his motivation, began to skip classes, and developed a reputation as a troublemaker.

His parents decided to move him to the co-educational Mount Temple High School, one of Ireland's first non-religious schools. Though he was still academically restless, he thrived socially and found stimulation among a group of creative and rebellious friends. Together they invented an "alternative community" that they called Lypton Village. "[We] used to put on arts installations, when we were 16, 17, with manic drills and step ladders," Bono said. "We invented our own language, gave each other names, and we'd dress differently." It was from a Lypton Village friend that Bono got his distinctive nickname, which is short for "Bono Vox." The friend lifted the name from a hearing-aid store in Dublin. At the time, Bono didn't realize that the phrase is an approximation of "good voice" in Latin, the language of the ancient Romans—a fitting name for a future singer.

After he graduated from Mount Temple, Bono enrolled briefly at the National University of Ireland to study English and history. But he was thrown out. "I had falsely matriculated [graduated], they told me. In National University, you are supposed to speak the national language, and I didn't," he recalled. "I had flunked Irish [language classes], and they found that out."

CAREER HIGHLIGHTS

Bono gained fame and respect as the lead singer and lyricist for U2, one of the world's most popular rock bands. He is known for his impassioned singing style and for the spiritual foundation of many of his lyrics. Though not openly Christian, many of his songs center on messages of peace, harmony, and fellowship—foundations of the Christian faith. In addition, in the late 1990s, Bono began to promote humanitarian causes. His political work on behalf of developing nations and the poor has won him praise and awards.

— " —

"We walked up on stage; I was playing guitar, and when I heard that D chord, I got some kick," Bono said about the band's first gig. "It was like four blind kids blustering away and there was evidence of just a little light in the corner and we started to work towards that. We built ourselves around that spark."

Forming a Band

Bono has been part of the band that became U2 since he was just a teenager. When he was 16, he responded to a notice on the school bulletin board posted by Larry Mullen Jr., a fellow student and drummer looking for musicians to form a rock band. Only he and three others turned up at the first meeting: Adam Clayton, who brought a bass guitar, an amp, and a sense of self-confidence that was much bigger than his musical ability; Dave Evans, an experienced guitarist who later adopted the name the Edge; and Evans's brother, Dick, who dropped out of the group in 1978.

Later, Mullen described the group's initial meeting to *Time* magazine music critic Jay Cocks: "The Edge could play. Adam just looked great. Big, bushy hair, long caftan coat, bass guitar, and amp. He talked like he could play, used all the right words, like gig. I thought, this guy must know how to play," he recalled. "Then Bono arrived, and he meant to play the guitar, but he couldn't play very well, so he started to sing. He couldn't do that either. But he was such a charismatic character that he was in the band anyway, as soon as he arrived. I was in charge for the first five minutes, but as soon as Bono got there, I was out of a job."

U2 performing at the US festival in California in 1983. Bono is in the center at the microphone, with the Edge on guitar on the left.

In spite of his show of confidence at the audition, Bono didn't think he could sing or play well enough to be in a band. But his doubts about his musical ability vanished in the thrill of performing. He told journalist Niall Stokes about the band's first gig: "We walked up on stage; I was playing guitar, and when I heard that D chord, I got some kick," he said. "It was like four blind kids blustering away and there was evidence of just a little light in the corner and we started to work towards that. We built ourselves around that spark."

In its early days, the band went by the names Feedback and The Hype before settling on U2, after an American military aircraft.

U2 Develops Its Songs and Style

Originally, the band members could barely play well enough to imitate other people's songs. So they began to compose their own. They developed an unusual process that has continued throughout their successful career: Bono or the Edge bring an idea to the group—a riff, a fragment of melody, or a phrase. Then Clayton and Mullen participate in actually building the song. In the process, the band tries to pinpoint a powerful, honest emotion or truth in the melody. Only then does Bono begin to work on composing lyrics.

According to Bono, he relies heavily on the emotion he first hears when experiencing the music. Bono told Richard Hilburn of the *Los Angeles Times* that he learned to be truthful from listening to John Lennon's solo albums. "He showed that the best way to unlock yourself as a writer was simply to tell the truth," Bono said. "When you've got a song to write or a blank page, just describe what is on your mind—not what you'd like to be on your mind. If you feel you have nothing to say, your first line then is, 'I have nothing to say.'"

Soon the band was composing songs that Hilburn described as "pop music at its most ambitious—personal and independent enough to satisfy discerning listeners, yet open and accessible enough to pack stadiums." The band also nurtured a distinctive sound driven by the Edge's signature guitar line, with a ringing sound played on the instrument's upper strings; Hilburn called it "the bright clarion cry of his guitar." Mullen and Clayton laid down an often-driving rhythm on bass and drums. Over it all, soared Bono's singing, which over time became powerful, passionate, and expressive. It soon became clear that Bono was the charismatic focus of the group. As *Time* magazine put it, "It is on Bono . . . that all eyes stay fixed. U2 carries the day, but he carries the show."

First Records

U2 had its first big break in a talent contest run by CBS Ireland. The company signed U2 and released a three-song EP (extended-play vinyl record) called *U2-3*. The disk topped the Irish charts and drew bigger crowds than ever to their live show. But CBS refused to issue the record outside of Ireland. Dissatisfied, Bono sent tapes to radio stations and journalists. In 1980 the band won a contract with Island Records, an independent English label known for backing new-wave groups.

U2 released it first album, *Boy*, in 1980, with songs that expressed the anger and energy of punk music. But instead of punk's nihilism, the songs hinted at hope and idealism. As the band's lyricist, Bono struck out at social and political injustice. "I Will Follow" had the anthem-like, almost religious quality that would mark much of U2's output. The critic Sean O'Hagan likened such songs to "rock hymns, their clarion calls riding on huge rolling guitar signatures." After the song was featured on the soundtrack of a movie called *The Last American Virgin*, U2 gained a key fan base in the United States.

A second album, *October* (1981), reflected conflict within the band. At the time, Bono had joined a Christian group and was struggling to reconcile his new rock-star role with a commitment to becoming a Christian.

Mullen and the Edge had similar conflicts. Meanwhile, Clayton just wanted to get on with rock, where his heart lay. The band members became somewhat estranged. "We were, during *October*, interested in other things, really," Bono said. "We were getting involved in reading books, the Big Book [the Bible], meeting people who were far more interested in things spiritual."

War

The band members managed to overcome their personal differences and produced their breakthrough album, *War*, in 1983. Riding on the success of *October*, it entered the sales charts at No. 1 in the United Kingdom. On the strength of several memorable songs, it also made the Top 10 in the United States. The surging emotional power of "I Will Follow" returned in "New Year's Day," a stinging anti-war piece. Politics took center stage in the hard-hitting "Sunday Bloody Sunday." The song centers on a 1972 incident in Northern Ireland when British paratroopers fired on unruly protest marchers, killing 13 people. Critics noted that U2 managed to oppose the violence of modern Ireland in the song without taking sides.

"More than any other record, *War* is right for its time," Bono said at the time. "It is a slap in the face against the snap, crackle, and pop. Everyone else is getting more and more style-orientated, more and more slick. John Lennon was right about that kind of music; he called it 'wallpaper music.' Very pretty, very well designed, music to eat your breakfast to. Music can be more. Its possibilities are great. Music has changed me. It has the ability to change a generation. Look at what happened with Vietnam. Music changed a whole generation's attitude towards war."

"

"More than any other record, War *is right for its time," Bono said. "It is a slap in the face against the snap, crackle, and pop. Everyone else is getting more and more style-orientated, more and more slick. John Lennon was right about that kind of music; he called it 'wallpaper music.' Very pretty, very well designed, music to eat your breakfast to."*

"

With the release of *War*, U2 began to get noticed for its strong political message as well as its distinctive, dense, layered sound. In a time of superficial pop music, U2 was welcomed as a throwback to the 1960s, when politics and social change were key elements of rock music. Also fueling the band's success was the airplay it received on MTV, which was just getting started at that time as a music video network. Bono's energy and magnetism in the video single for "New Year's Day" attracted many fans. The band soon sealed its status as a global phenomenon with the release of a live album and concert video, both called *Under a Blood-Red Sky* (1983).

With the release of its fourth album, *The Unforgettable Fire* (1984), U2 switched producers, from Steve Lilywhite to the more experimental Brian Eno and Daniel Lanois. New elements came into their music, including jazz-influenced instrumental sections. *The Unforgettable Fire* drew the most negative reviews of the band's career to date. But it also enjoyed huge success with the single "Pride (In the Name of Love)," a tribute to the American civil rights leader Martin Luther King Jr. In 1985, rock magazine *Rolling Stone* named U2 "the band of the 1980s."

Becoming an Activist

Following the popularity of *War,* U2 had been invited to perform in Live Aid, the pioneering rock concerts organized by Bob Geldof. The effort raised $200 million for famine victims in Africa. His involvement with African issues inspired Bono to spend six weeks with his wife Alison in Ethiopia in 1985, working at a refugee camp. This initial involvement would later grow into his high-profile lobbying for African and third-world causes. Years later, Bono told a church congregation that his activism started with his trip to Ethiopia. "It's a journey that changed my life forever," he said.

In the meantime, Bono and the band got involved in other political crusades. U2 contributed to a Sun City album with other musicians to raise money to fight racist policies in South Africa. They also headlined a tour with other artists in 1986 to benefit Amnesty International, a group that fights human-rights abuses worldwide. In interviews and even onstage, Bono began to comment on these issues and other political matters, including the violence in Northern Ireland and America. Reactions to his activism were mixed: some disliked what they regarded as his air of pompousness and self-importance, while others appreciated his passion and commitment.

The Joshua Tree

In *The Joshua Tree,* released in 1987, Bono and the band focused on American politics. The critic Niall Stokes noted that the album expresses the "sense of outrage that America's unique combination of arrogance and apathy inspires from an Irish perspective." Bono and the band used as their central image the Joshua Tree, a species that thrives in the southwestern American desert. Critics saw the plant as representing the human idealism and compassion that can blossom even in the barren desert of contemporary American power politics. "A lot of the songs were ones that were recorded in Larry's spare bedroom or Adam's living room. When the red light's on we often don't respond to it. When we're just left to be, left to make music our own way, well some of the tracks are almost like demos. We had to fight to make them work and there were a lot of songs left over. It could have gone off in a number of different directions. We wanted the idea of a one-piece record, not a side-one, side-two thing."

The Joshua Tree became the album that catapulted the group to super-stardom. Two of the album's singles, "With or Without You" and "I Still Haven't Found What I'm Looking For," became No. 1 hits in the United States—U2's first U.S. top hits. *Time* magazine put the band on its cover and pro-

claimed it "Rock's Hottest Ticket." At the 1988 Grammy Awards, *The Joshua Tree* earned U2 the award for best performance by a rock group and album of the year award. The band was at this time acknowledged as the most popular and powerful rock band in the world. "This is the album that will catapult U2 from cult status to worldwide superstardom," Daniel Brogan wrote in the *Chicago Tribune*. "The only question is how they will deal with it. My guess is that U2 will be remembered as the most influential band of the late '80s and early '90s."

"[The album is] a masterpiece, a work of profound elegance and mystery and faith," wrote Robert Hilburn of the *Los Angeles Times*. "In *The Joshua Tree,* U2 fills in the sketches with sometimes breathtaking signs of growth. The music . . . is more tailored and assured as it expands on the moody textures of songs like "Bad" and reaches out with great effect for new, bluesy touches. . . . In a time when the rock 'n' roll world feasts on the banality of such acts as Bon Jovi, *The Joshua Tree* is asking more of mainstream audiences than any pop-rock album since Bruce Springsteen's *Nebraska*. [And] the band presents its case in such majestic, heartfelt and accessible terms. . . . *The Joshua Tree* finally confirms on record what this band has been slowly asserting for three years now on stage: U2 is what the Rolling Stones ceased being years ago—the greatest rock 'n' roll band in the world. In this album, the band wears that mantle securely."

After the great success of *The Joshua Tree,* Bono and U2 set out on a journey of musical discovery across America. They visited the American South to find the roots of rock and roll in such styles as Appalachian folk music, African-American gospel, the blues of artists like Robert Johnson, and the jazz of singers like Billie Holiday and others. They also explored country music, from early artists like Hank Williams to more recent stars like Johnny Cash. The tour included a stop at Sun Studios in Memphis, Tennessee, where Elvis Presley and Johnny Cash got their start. The group also collaborated with music legends like B.B. King and Bob Dylan, who co-wrote "Love Rescue Me."

"

***"The Joshua Tree** finally confirms on record what this band has been slowly asserting for three years now on stage: U2 is what the Rolling Stones ceased being years ago—the greatest rock 'n' roll band in the world. In this album, the band wears that mantle securely."*

—Robert Hilburn, the **Los Angeles Times**

"

These experiences were presented in a black-and-white documentary film called *Rattle and Hum,* which was released in 1988 along with an album of the same name. The record was a success with such hits as "Desire," and some critics praised the disk's energy and daring. But some reviewers and fans thought the Irish rockers were presumptuous to suggest they could reveal insights about American music.

Achtung Baby

Between 1988 and 1990, Bono and the band took a break from recording. They came back in 1991 with *Achtung Baby,* recorded over several months in Berlin, Germany. The Edge said that with this album, the band was "smashing U2 and starting all over again." Instead of politics, the album explored the darker themes of disappointed love and sexual jealousy. The band experimented with electronic elements that added a new edge to their music—for example, Bono used devices like distortion pedals to make his tenor voice sound lower. The ballad, "One," is a signature song from the record.

"At their best, these Irishmen have proven—just as Springsteen and the Who did—that the same penchant for epic musical and verbal gestures that leads many artists to self-parody can, in more inspired hands, fuel the unforgettable fire that defines great rock & roll," Elyse Gardner wrote in *Rolling Stone*. "In the past, U2's frontman has turned out fiercely pointed social and political diatribes, but his more confessional and romantic songs, however felt, have been evasive. On *Achtung*, though, Bono deals more directly with his private feelings. . . . That's not to say that U2 has forsaken its faith or that Bono has abandoned his quest to find what he's looking for. On the radiant ballad 'One,' the band invests an unexceptional message— 'We're one/But we're not the same/We get to carry each other'—with such urgency that it sounds like a revelation. Few bands can marshal such sublime power."

"

Daniel Brogan wrote in the **Chicago Tribune**, *"My guess is that U2 will be remembered as the most influential band of the late '80s and early '90s."*

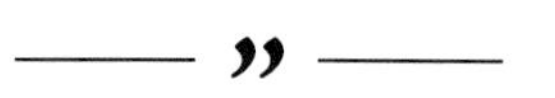

The Zoo TV tour that the band launched with the album also showed a new side to U2. Instead of their usual stripped-down stages, they devised a concert set where cars hung from the ceiling and gigantic TV screens displayed messages and video. Bono himself also began to adopt extreme stage personas during this period, including Fly, a leather-clad hoodlum; the Mirrorball man, a take-off on TV evangelists; and Mister MacPhisto (a play on the devil's name, Mephisto), who wore a gold-lame suit and was a combination of middle-aged Elvis and Lucifer himself. Offstage, Bono began to wear the wrap-around sunglasses that have become his trademark.

Between the close of the Zoo TV tour in late 1992 and the start of the European tour in May 1993, U2 paused to put together a "mini-album," *Zooropa*. But it soon grew into a full-length recording, with songs that often ventured into techno-dance music. Critics generally approved of the experimental and spontaneous results. But some reviewers agreed with a *People* magazine commentator, who wrote that "some of these songs needed more planning and polishing."

The members of U2 (left to right): the Edge, Bono, Adam Clayton, and Larry Mullens.

In 1997, U2 re-emerged as a dance-rock band in the album *Pop*. Howie B., a techno producer and performer, brought convincing credentials to the project. It received mixed reviews. But when the band took the show on the road for the Pop tour, it met with a lukewarm reception. With elaborate props, including a 35-foot-tall mirror ball, the tour cost about $250,000 a day, and with tickets selling poorly, the band barely broke even.

All That You Can't Leave Behind

Fans responded more warmly when Bono and U2 greeted the new millennium with *All That You Can't Leave Behind* (2000), a nod to their 1980s roots. "Pop music often tells you everything is OK, while rock music tells you that it's not OK, but you can change it," Bono said about the record.

"There's a defiance in rock music that gives you a reason to get out of bed in the morning. Most pop music doesn't make you want to get out of bed, I'm sorry to say. It puts you to sleep."

Songs like the hit "Beautiful Day" returned to the guitar-propelled simpler sound of the band's earliest hits. After the terrorist attacks on New York and Washington DC on September 11, 2001, many fans adopted the album's song "Walk On" as an anthem of hope and perseverance. Although the song was released before the attacks occurred, many found that its lyrics spoke directly to the moment. During their 2001 Elevation tour after September 11, the band paid tribute to the victims and heroes of the attacks by projecting their names on large screens during their performances. U2 was chosen to perform at the 2002 NFL Super Bowl before a huge live crowd and an appreciative TV audience. That year the band earned four Grammy awards.

——— “ ———

"Pop music often tells you everything is OK, while rock music tells you that it's not OK, but you can change it," Bono said. "There's a defiance in rock music that gives you a reason to get out of bed in the morning. Most pop music doesn't make you want to get out of bed, I'm sorry to say. It puts you to sleep."

"On *All That You Can't Leave Behind,* U2 distills two decades of music-making into the illusion of effortlessness usually only possible from veterans," wrote *Rolling Stone*. "The album represents the most uninterrupted collection of strong melodies U2 [has] ever mounted. . . . *All That You Can't Leave Behind* flexes with an interior fire. Every track—whether reflective but swinging, like 'Wild Honey,' or poised, then pouncing, like 'Beautiful Day'—honors a tune so refined that each seems like some durable old number. Because this is U2, there's a quick impact to these melodies, yet each song has a resonance that doesn't fade with repeated listening. . . . Bono's singing has lost some of the extra flamboyance it's had in the past, but it's as passionate as ever—by reining himself in, he has invested his voice with a new urgency."

A Leading Humanitarian Activist

During the 1990s, Bono and U2 continued to support political causes. They contributed songs to albums released to fund education about AIDS. Their 1992 tour ended with a benefit concert for the ecology-minded charity

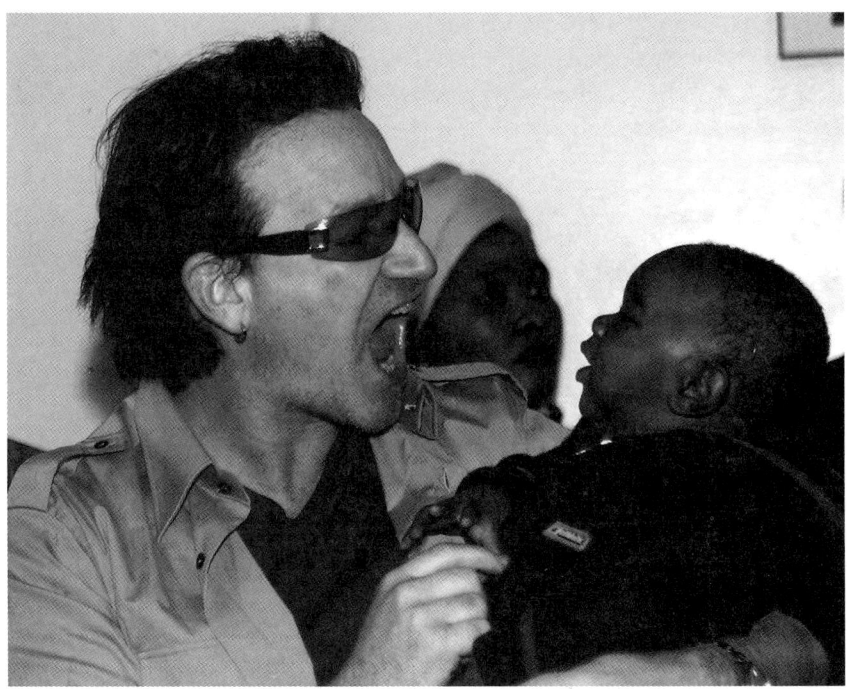

Bono's work as an activist has included several trips to Africa. On this visit to South Africa in 2002, he visited an HIV clinic at a hospital in Soweto.

Greenpeace, which incorporated a protest about nuclear power in the United Kingdom.

While Bono was interested in a variety of political causes, activism remained in the background of his life. That changed in 1997 when an advocate for African development, Jamie Drummond, contacted Bono with a stark statistic: Live Aid raised $200 million to help Africa. But that was a drop in the bucket compared to the loan payments that burdened most African countries. Countries would borrow money to pay for crucial expenses, but many African nations were too poor to pay back those loans. For example, Ethiopia was obliged to pay $500 million every year to banks to repay its debts. Drummond wanted Bono to get involved with Jubilee 2000, a campaign that asked governments to mark the new millennium by canceling debt for third-world countries. Bono soon agreed to become a spokesman for the cause.

But Bono wasn't satisfied to become a mere figurehead. He began to fly to Washington DC to learn everything he could about the economics of Africa. He discovered that Congress, not the president, had the power to erase African debt. So he began to lobby members of Congress—Democrats, Republicans, across the board. It took a while for him to be taken seriously, but it only took one meeting for even the biggest skeptics to see that Bono knew his stuff. According to Bill O'Reilly, a conservative American news commentator, "I think Bono should win the Nobel Peace Prize. He's not a phony." That view was echoed by Paul Wolfowitz, president of the World Bank: "Pomposity and arrogance are the enemies of getting things done. And Bono knows how to get things done."

"They really are a group, the only real group I've ever met," Brian Eno, the noted composer, musician, and producer, said about U2. "They realize that intuitively, and there is a great loyalty, perhaps because they realize that none of them would have been a musician without the others."

Bono quickly developed a reputation as a knowledgeable humanitarian. He was soon welcomed by the world's most prominent politicians and world leaders, from Presidents Bill Clinton and George W. Bush, to South African former President Nelson Mandela, to Pope John Paul II (who reportedly tried on Bono's sunglasses). Often his meetings got results—for example, the Jubilee 2000 campaign was a success. And partly due to Bono's influence, Bush launched programs to give drugs to poor Africans suffering from HIV. The president also released funds to developing governments, on the condition that they agreed to accountability standards.

In 2002, Bono co-founded DATA—Debts, AIDS, Trade in Africa—a nonprofit organization devoted to his favorite causes. Bono didn't want people to think it was a "vanity" project, so he found grants to fund it instead of paying for it himself. Bono emphasized that the group is not just for fund-raising, but also for organizing a real movement to create political change. "Each generation has to ask itself what it wants to be remembered for. Previous generations have ushered in civil rights in America, gotten rid of apartheid in South Africa, and brought down the iron curtain," he said. "I think this generation can bring that kind of energy and conviction to the problems in Africa."

In July 2005, Bono helped to organize Live 8, a series of free international concerts designed to raise the profile of the issues of debt forgiveness, fair trade, and financial aid to Africa. The concerts took place at the same time as the G-8 summit—a forum where leaders representing the world's wealthiest countries were meeting to discuss common issues. Bono and DATA reps met with five of the eight leaders and helped influence the group to approve $50 billion in aid. The leaders also promised antiretroviral drugs for millions of poor people with HIV. They cancelled the debt of 18 of the poorest African countries. Bono didn't do it on his own, said Paul Martin, prime minister of Canada. "But it's hard to imagine much of it would have been done without him," he said.

In 2005, Bono was nominated for the Nobel Peace Prize and was named Person of the Year by *Time* magazine (along with Microsoft billionaires and fellow activists Bill Gates and Melinda Gates) for his work on behalf of Africa. Also in 2005, Bono helped launch the Red label in partnership with such companies as Gap, Converse, American Express, and Giorgio Armani. Red products are made in Africa from African resources. One percent of the profits from their sales go to the Global Fund to Fight AIDS, Tuberculosis, and Malaria.

A Rock-Solid Band

In addition to his work as an activist, Bono remains committed to U2. The band displayed its extraordinary staying power, nearly 30 years after forming, with the 2004 release of *How to Dismantle an Atomic Bomb*. The best-selling album yielded such major hits as "Vertigo" and "Sometimes You Can't Make It on Your Own," a tribute to the singer's father, who died in 2001. It also spawned the highly successful Vertigo tour, where fans of many ages confirmed their devotion to the group.

Critics, too, were quick to express their appreciation for the new work. "*How to Dismantle an Atomic Bomb* is the catchiest album U2 has ever made. Mostly it's perfectly rendered grandiose pop, enormous in sound and theme," Josh Tyrangiel wrote in *Time*. Reviewer Chuck Arnold agreed, writing in *People* magazine, "After a mid-career slump (*Pop*, anyone?), U2 reclaimed its title as the World's Greatest Rock Band with 2000's smashing comeback *All That You Can't Leave Behind*, which found Bono, the Edge, and company going back to what they do best: anthemic rock that elevates you to a higher place. Having reignited their unforgettable fire, they keep the fuse burning brightly on *How to Dismantle an Atomic Bomb*, another vintage U2 album." Writing in *Billboard* magazine, critic Wayne Robins had this to say: "*How to Dismantle an Atomic Bomb* is quintessential U2, taken to the next level," Robins wrote. "The sound is bigger, the playing better, the lyrics sharper, and the spirituality more compelling than anything the act has done in many years. . . . The Edge has never played with greater confidence, . . . and Bono's mature phrasing puts his well-crafted words across

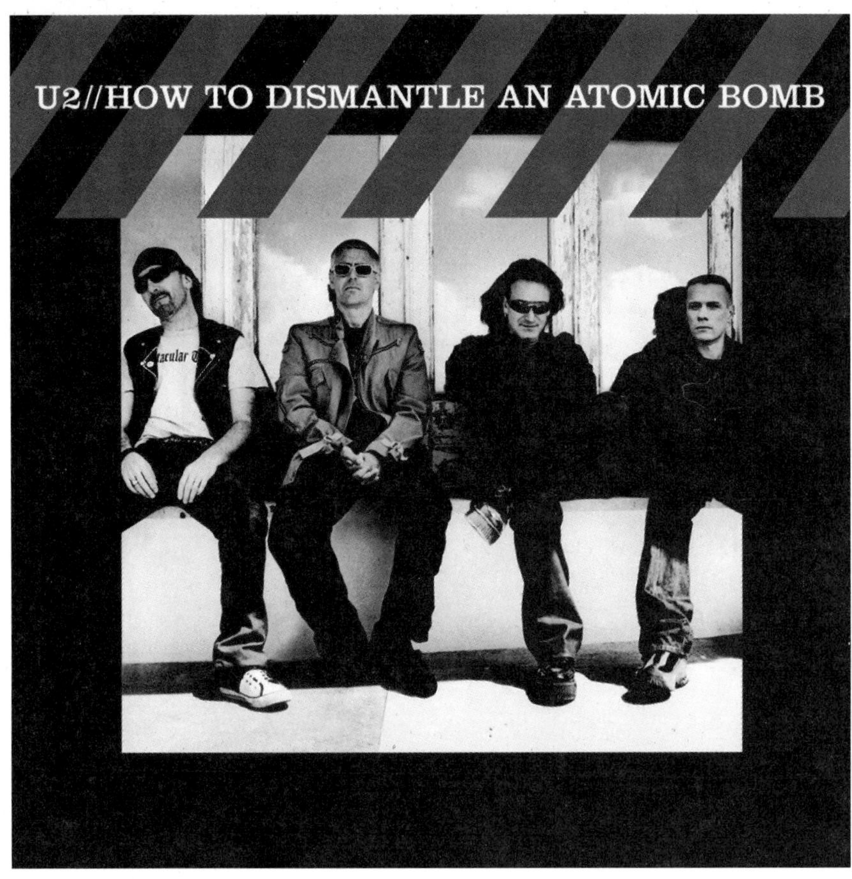

with conviction. Songwriting may be the most impressive part of a record on which U2 scales new peaks: . . . the album is full of great songs, performed with the vitality of a band that keeps surprising us by simply being itself."

Indeed, the commitment of the members of U2—to their music and to each other—is remarkable in the fast-changing music world. According to Brian Eno, the noted composer, musician, and producer, "They really are a group, the only real group I've ever met. They realize that intuitively, and there is a great loyalty, perhaps because they realize that none of them would have been a musician without the others."

Bono's commitment to rock music hasn't changed either after all these years. "Rock music can change things. I know that it changed our lives," he declared. "Rock is really about the transcendent feeling. There's life in the form. I still think that rock music is the only music that can still get you to that eternal place where you want to start a revolution, call your mother, change your job, or change your mind. I think that's what rock music can do."

"Rock music can change things. I know that it changed our lives," Bono declared. "Rock is really about the transcendent feeling. There's life in the form. I still think that rock music is the only music that can still get you to that eternal place where you want to start a revolution, call your mother, change your job, or change your mind. I think that's what rock music can do."

MARRIAGE AND FAMILY

Bono married his high-school sweetheart, Alison Stewart, in 1982. "It's almost impossible to be married and be in a band on the road, but Ali is able to make it work," Bono said. The couple has four children, Jordan, Eve, Elijah, and John. Bono told Oprah Winfrey in 2003, "I don't know why I have the life I have. I don't deserve it. I think the family is as strong as it is because of my wife, Ali. She is just really so cool."

The family lives outside Dublin, Ireland, where Bono says he can exist "below the celebrity radar." He is never away from his family for more than a few weeks. "You may get the impression I'm always out there, but I'm usually home driving my kids to school," he said. Bono and his family also spend time at their homes in New York City and the south of France.

HOBBIES AND OTHER INTERESTS

Bono is an avid reader. He has found inspiration for his songs in everything from biblical scriptures to the works of the American writers Flannery O'Connor and Charles Bukowski.

SELECTED RECORDINGS (with U2)

Boy, 1980
October, 1981
War, 1983
Under a Blood-Red Sky, 1983
The Unforgettable Fire, 1984
Wide Awake in America, 1985

The Joshua Tree, 1987
Rattle and Hum, 1988
Achtung Baby, 1991
Zooropa, 1993
Pop, 1997
Best of U2 1980-1990, 1998
All That You Can't Leave Behind, 2000
Best of U2 1990-2000, 2002
How to Dismantle an Atomic Bomb, 2004

SELECTED HONORS AND AWARDS (with U2)

Grammy Awards, with U2: 1987 (two awards), for album of the year and best rock vocal performance by a duo or group, both for *The Joshua Tree*; 1988 (two awards), for best rock vocal performance by a duo or group, for *"Desire"* and best performance in a music video, for "Where the Streets Have No Name"; 1992, for best rock vocal performance by a duo or group, for *Achtung Baby*; 1993, for best alternative music album, for *Zooropa*; 1994, for best music video, long form, for *Zoo TV: Live from Sydney*; 2000 (three awards), for record of the year, song of the year, and best rock vocal performance by a duo or group, all for "Beautiful Day"; 2001 (four awards), for best pop vocal performance by a duo or group for "Stuck in a Moment That You Can't Get Out Of," best rock vocal performance by a duo or group for "Elevation," record of the year for "Walk On," and best rock album, for *All That You Can't Leave Behind*; 2004 (three awards), for best rock vocal performance by a duo or group, best rock song, and best short-form music video, all for "Vertigo"; 2005 (five awards), for album of the year and best rock album, both for *How to Dismantle an Atomic Bomb*, song of the year and best rock vocal performance by a duo or group, both for "Sometimes You Can't Make It on Your Own," and best rock song, for "City of Blinding Lights"
British Record Industry Awards, with U2: Best International Group: 1988, 1989, 1990, 1998, 2001; Outstanding Contribution to the Record Industry, 2001; Most Successful Live Act, 1993
Humanitarian Laureate Award (Simon Wiesenthal Center): 2002
Humanitarian Award (Martin Luther King Jr. Center): 2003
Salute to Greatness Award (Martin Luther King Jr. Center): 2004
Ambassador of Conscience (Amnesty International): 2005
Inducted into the Rock and Roll Hall of Fame: 2005 (with U2)
Order of Liberty (President of Portugal): 2005 (with U2)
Person of the Year (*Time* magazine): 2005 (with Bill and Melinda Gates)
Pablo Neruda Arts Award (President of Chile): 2006

FURTHER READING

Books

Assayas, Michka. *Bono: Conversations with Michka Assayas*, 2005
Dunphy, Eamon. *Unforgettable Fire*, 1988
Encyclopedia of World Biography Supplement, Vol. 24, 2005
Jackson, Laura. *Bono: His Life, Music, and Passions*, 2001
Parkyn, Geoff. *Touch the Flame*, 1988
Who's Who in America, 2006

Periodicals

Christian Century, Mar. 21, 2006, pp.20 and 23
Christianity Today, Mar. 2003, p.38
Current BiographyYearbook, 1993
Los Angeles Times, June 6, 2002, p.14; Aug. 8, 2004, p.1
Newsweek, Jan. 24, 2000, p.58
O: The Oprah Magazine, Apr. 2004, p.195
Rolling Stone, Oct. 8, 1987, p.43; Nov. 3, 2005, p.48
Time, Mar. 4, 2002, p.62; Apr. 27, 1987, p.72; Sep. 15, 2001, p.52; Dec. 26, 2005, pp.38, 46, and 65; May 8, 2006, p.116
Vogue, Mar. 2005, p.524
Washington Post, Sep. 20, 1987, p.1

Online Databases

Biography Resource Center Online, 2006, article from *Encyclopedia of World Biography Supplement*, 2005
Wilson Web, 2006, article from *Current Biography: World Musicians*, 1993, updated 1998

ADDRESS

Bono
Universal Music Group
1755 Broadway
New York, NY 10019

WORLD WIDE WEB SITES

http://www.u2.com
http://www.data.org

BRIEF ENTRY

Kelsie Buckley 1995-

American Student
Fundraiser for Hurricane-Damaged Libraries and Large-Print Books

EARLY YEARS

Kelsie Buckley was born on March 11, 1995, in Houston, Texas, to Kelly and Thomas Buckley. Her father is a self-employed welder. In the first years of her life, the family traveled through Texas and California as her father worked at different jobs.

When she was four Kelsie could read at a second-grade level, according to her mother. At that same young age, she became interested in the political process. "She wanted to know everything about elections and how the government works," explained her mother.

Kelsie attended kindergarten at O.M. Roberts Elementary School in Lake Jackson, Texas. One day, when recess was cut back 15 minutes for an assembly, she staged a sit-in at school. "She just wrapped her arms around a pole and refused to come inside because it was too early," her mother recalled. "It was kind of funny! But after that, we talked to her about it being all right to ask questions, but you have to be polite and respectful. She learned that lesson real quick."

The Buckleys moved to Benicia, California, when Kelsie was in first grade, and then settled in Morton, Mississippi, about a year later. She became a home-schooled student, with her mother as her teacher. Kelsie was an avid reader, getting through two or three chapter books a week. She loved adventure books as well as history books. One of her favorite subjects was Benjamin Franklin.

Onset of Vision Problems

In June 2004, when Kelsie was nine years old, she began to notice that the words in books looked fuzzy. In a few short weeks, she could not see the print at all and her eyes became very sensitive to light. Her eyes burned "like when you touch a heater that's been on a long time," she said.

"

When Kelsie was nine years old, she began to notice that the words in books looked fuzzy. In a few short weeks, she could not see the print at all and her eyes became very sensitive to light. Her eyes burned "like when you touch a heater that's been on a long time," she said.

Her parents took Kelsie to many eye doctors, but they could not agree on what was wrong. Finally, a pediatric eye specialist from Los Angeles diagnosed her problem as ocular histoplasmosis syndrome. It is a disease caused by a fungus that scars and inflames the retina and can, in some cases, lead to permanent blindness. In October 2005, the specialist operated on Kelsie. The operation made her eyes less sensitive to light. She has no vision in her left eye and has limited vision in her right eye. She was fitted with special glasses that help her get around by herself and watch television. But she could not read books unless the letters were printed in type about twice the normal size.

The size of the letters in books, magazines and newspapers is measured in points. The typical print size is about 10 or 12 points (like the size of the print in this book). By the time she turned nine, Kelsie could no longer read 12-point type. She went to the Morton Public Library, near her home, to take out large print books. The Morton library, like most libraries in the United States, has a small collection of large print books. But the print in those books is usually 16-point type, which is still too small for Kelsie. She could read them with a magnifying glass, but her arm got tired after a few pages. She needed books that were printed in 20-point type or larger. But the only way to get them was for her parents to buy them for her, and they were very expensive.

"My first goal was to raise enough money for 200 books, [and] that would come to around $4,000," Kelsie said. "After I reached my goal, I donated 12 inches of my hair to a child that had gone through chemotherapy. I had never gotten a haircut before, but I was excited about helping others."

MAJOR ACCOMPLISHMENTS

First Fund-Raising Campaign

Determined to help children with vision problems, Kelsie decided to take action. She began a fund-raising effort, asking people to donate money so the Morton Public Library could buy books with 20-point type. "My first goal was to raise enough money for 200 books, [and] that would come to around $4,000," Kelsie said on her web site, http://www.kelsiesbooks.net. "After I reached my goal, I donated 12 inches of my hair to a child that had gone through chemotherapy. I had never gotten a haircut before, but I was excited about helping others."

Kelsie also began writing letters to elected officials in Mississippi, as well as President George W. Bush. She knew that in 2001 the U.S. Congress had passed the Elementary and Secondary Education Act (often called the "No Child Left Behind" Act). President George W. Bush had supported the bill, which set high standards for the learning of all children, regardless of their background or ability. Kelsie wrote to the president, telling him, "You said no child left behind. I am telling you that I feel left behind. . . . Please write back so I can tell you my plan, but not after 8:30 because that is my bedtime."

In February 2005, nine-year-old Kelsie spoke at a hearing of the House Public Health Committee at the Mississippi House of Representatives. "I

Hurricane Katrina wreaked devastation on schools and libraries, as shown in this 2005 photo of the Gorenflo Elementary School library in Gulfport, Mississippi.

think that it is sad that I am an American child and I can't go to my local library and check out a book to read," she said.

Kelsie received telephone calls of support from a staff member of the office of First Lady Laura Bush, as well as staffers in the offices of U.S. Sen. Thad Cochran of Mississippi and Mississippi Governor Haley Barbour. U.S. Rep. Chip Pickering called Kelsie himself. She asked them all to back her plan: to make funds available so all low-vision children can get any book they want at the type-size they need. "They all promised to help," said her mother, Kelly Buckley. "And Kelsie made sure to keep calling them back, just to check up on them and keep them to their word!"

Hurricane Katrina

In August 2005, Hurricane Katrina slammed into the coasts of Louisiana and Mississippi. One of the tornadoes spawned by the storm hit Kelsie's hometown of Morton. She and her parents huddled in the bathtub as the tornado approached because the bathroom was the central room in the house and there were no windows. "I was really scared," she recalled. "It felt like our house was a small rowboat and a big wave was coming over us."

Fortunately, the family was not hurt, but their house was wrecked. There were no hotel rooms available, so the family camped out, sharing food and supplies with their neighbors. They later moved in with friends in Jackson, Mississippi. They went to Florida next, but were soon hit by Hurricane Wilma in October 2005. "After Hurricane Wilma hit Florida, we'd had enough," Kelly Buckley said. "We called FEMA." The Federal Emergency Management Agency (FEMA) is an agency of the federal government that manages the government's response to natural disasters. FEMA offers assistance, including temporary housing, to victims of national disasters. Because so many people were left homeless in the wake of Hurricane Katrina and the other Atlantic storms of 2005, FEMA commissioned cruise ships to provide shelter to some victims. The Buckleys lived for eight weeks on a ship docked in Pascagoula, Mississippi.

"During Hurricane Katrina, one of the tornadoes spawned by the storm hit Kelsie's hometown. She and her parents huddled in the bathtub as the tornado approached because the bathroom was the central room in the house and there were no windows. "I was really scared," she recalled. "It felt like our house was a small rowboat and a big wave was coming over us.""

Kelsie's Book Trail Ride

Despite the upheaval in her life, Kelsie did not forget about her book campaign. "Kelsie begged from the time we got on the ship to go see the libraries," her mother recalled. As it turned out, there were no libraries near her home to see. Seven libraries in Mississippi, including the Morton library, were destroyed by Hurricane Katrina.

A week before Christmas 2005, the Buckleys moved into a house trailer provided by FEMA. Kelsie began planning a new fund-raising campaign. Her goal was not just raising money for large-print books anymore. Now she also wanted to help fix the seven damaged libraries for the sake of all the area's children, according to her mother. "Kelsie realized that you need a building before you need books," Kelly Buckley said.

For Christmas that year, Kelsie had gotten a horse she named Chester. On March 2, 2006, she climbed onto Chester to begin Kelsie's Book Trail Ride. She and her parents led supporters on horseback and in buggies on a 10-day journey from Morton to Gulfport, Mississippi. Kelsie wanted to raise

Buckley and First Lady Laura Bush being interviewed by reporter Steve Hartman for CBS News.

$10,000 for each of the seven damaged libraries. The caravan stopped in towns along the way to collect money from local residents. The ride, which ended on her 11th birthday, raised $9,000 and generated a lot of publicity.

On March 31, 2006, Kelsie appeared on national TV on the "CBS Evening News." The reporter, Steve Hartman, asked her what it was about books that motivated her to act. "Books are to help you get your mind off the bad things that are going on," she said. Hartman also asked if she would feel mad if she went completely blind from her eye disease and couldn't see any books. "No sir, I wouldn't be mad," Kelsie replied. "Actually, I'd just—I might cry, but I would still keep on going."

After Kelsie appeared on television, thousands of people from across the United States and around the world logged on to her web site and made donations. In less than a month, she raised almost $80,000, which she gave to state library officials. She also passed along the numerous autographed books that authors sent her. Kelsie said that she planned to "start all over again" and raise another $70,000 for Mississippi libraries.

Soon after the CBS report aired, First Lady Laura Bush, who is a former librarian, called Kelsie. The first lady invited Kelsie to be her guest when she traveled to Biloxi, Mississippi, to award grants from the Laura Bush Foundation to help school libraries restock their books. During a speech in

Biloxi on May 3, 2006, Bush thanked Kelsie for all her efforts. One of the dignitaries attending the speech was Ann Moore, the chairman and CEO of Time Inc., who donated $20,000 to Kelsie's library campaign. The first lady and Kelsie were later interviewed together by Steve Hartman of CBS. Asked why she became interested in Kelsie, Laura Bush replied, "Well, of course it was because she loves books. And she wanted schools to have books and libraries to have books. That's what I like to do. And when I was Kelsie's age, that was my favorite thing to do—read."

"

Asked why she became interested in Kelsie, First Lady Laura Bush replied, "Well, of course it was because she loves books. And she wanted schools to have books and libraries to have books. That's what I like to do. And when I was Kelsie's age, that was my favorite thing to do—read."

"

By spring 2006, the Buckley family had moved out of the FEMA trailer, which had a leaky roof, and into their own travel trailer, which can be pulled by a truck. In late May 2006, Kelsie and her parents traveled to Johns Hopkins Hospital in Baltimore, Maryland, for an examination by eye specialists there. After her examination, Kelsie and her parents went to the White House, at the invitation of First Lady Laura Bush. The Buckleys also met with President George W. Bush. "It was cool to meet the president," Kelsie said. "He told me that I was doing a great job and that I was an inspiration for all kids in America."

HOBBIES AND OTHER INTERESTS

When she isn't working on her library campaign, Kelsie likes to spend her time reading, collecting rocks, riding her horse, riding her bicycle, and swimming. She also likes to paint pictures, using oils or pastel chalks. When asked if she has difficulty seeing what she's drawing, Kelsie replied, "You see with your heart."

FURTHER READING

Periodicals

Biloxi (MS) Sun Herald, Feb. 18, 2005, p.A4; Mar. 7, 2006, p.B1; May 2, 2006, p.A4; May 4, 2006, p.A1

Hattiesburg (MS) American, Mar. 5, 2005, p.C1

Online Articles

http://www.cbsnews.com/stories/2006/03/31/eveningnews/main1461732.shtml
(CBS News, "Seeing Life Clearly: 11-Year-Old with Vision Trouble Raises Money to Rebuild Katrina-Ravaged Libraries," Mar. 31, 2006)
http://www.cbsnews.com/stories/2006/05/04/eveningnews/main1584977.shtml
(CBS News, "First Lady Meets First Bookworm: Laura Bush Goes to Mississippi to Thank Extraordinary 11-Year-Old," May 4, 2006)

ADDRESS

Kelsie Buckley
Kelsie's Books
P.O. Box 506
Morton, MS 39117

WORLD WIDE WEB SITE

http://www.kelsiesbooks.net

Cynthia Kadohata 1956-

American Young Adult Novelist
Winner of the 2005 Newbery Medal for *Kira-Kira*

BIRTH

Cynthia Kadohata was born on July 2, 1956, in Chicago, Illinois. Her mother, Jane Akiko Kaita, was born in California and grew up in Hawaii. Her father, Toshiro Kadohata, grew up in California, where his parents were tenant farmers. Cynthia has an older sister and a younger brother.

During World War II, Toshiro Kadohata was interned along with his family and thousands of other Japanese-Americans in the Poston internment camp in Arizona. It was located on the Colorado River Indian Reservation in the Sonoran desert. At that time, the United States was at war with Japan. Some Americans worried that Japanese and Japanese-American people living and working in the U.S. might be traitors who would sabotage the American war effort—even though most thought of themselves as loyal Americans. President Franklin Delano Roosevelt ordered that people of Japanese descent should be evacuated from their homes and imprisoned in internment camps. Approximately 120,000 people, including Toshiro Kadohata, were confined to these internment camps. Later, he was drafted out of the camp and served with the U.S. Military Intelligence Service in Japan.

YOUTH

At the time of Kadohata's birth, her mother and father owned a small grocery store in Chicago. Her father decided to find a job in chicken sexing, which is the painstaking process of separating male chicks from female chicks. Chicken sexing was developed in Japan, and the men who practiced it were overwhelmingly Japanese and Japanese-American. After training, he was offered a job at a hatchery in Tifton, Georgia, where the family moved when Cynthia was two years old. Like the other chicken sexers, he often worked 100 hours a week, taking amphetamines to stay awake through the night.

When the hatchery closed, the family moved to Springdale, Arkansas, where they were the only nonwhite members of the local Presbyterian church. Kadohata recalls that she did not have many friends during this time. "We fit in by not fitting into it, by being part of a very small community," she said in an interview. "When we went to a party, it was almost always with a group of other Japanese or Japanese Americans who worked as chicken sexers, separating male and female chicks in the hatchery. I remember a little girl asking me something like, 'Are you black or white?' I really stumbled for an answer. I said, 'I don't know.'" After her brother was born, the entire hospital staff gathered to see him because no one in town had seen a Japanese baby before.

When Kadohata was young, her parents began to grow apart. "When my mother began taking us to the library, she discovered a love of reading at the same time we did," Kadohata said in her Newbery acceptance speech. "Someone once said to me, 'The problems between your parents began when your mother started reading.'" Despite the difficult times, there were also good times too. "One of my favorite childhood memories is of when my mother became obsessed with the stars. She made charts of the constellations and lay with us in the back yard at night to look at the clear skies of our small Arkansas town. One of the family activities I remember most vividly is burning our garbage together in the incinerator in back at night, the ashes sparkling through the air as the fire warmed our faces."

Kadohata's parents divorced when she was nine years old. Her father remained in Arkansas, but her mother moved with Cynthia and her siblings back to Chicago. The 1960s were an exciting time in the city, and Kadohata made the most of her time there. "I loved Chicago and the Sixties!" she remembered. "I loved Twiggy, the Beatles, the clothes. I loved Bobby Kennedy, and the night he died I slept on a concrete floor in our apartment and prayed and cried myself to sleep. Later . . . I loved secretly staying at the beach overnight with my friends." She had a lot of freedom as a teenager. "My mother worked full-time and went to school nights, taking the subway home and returning late to find us still awake," she wrote. "We were all three good students, and we were never punished, for anything."

EDUCATION

In 1972, when she was 16, Kadohata moved with her family to Los Angeles. She enrolled at Hollywood High School, but she ran into trouble right away. "I had gone to an alternative high school in Chicago, and Hollywood High wouldn't accept a lot of my credits," she stated. "But I also didn't fit in. I became intensely shy. It got to the point that going to the grocery store and talking to the cashier really made me nervous." A year later, at the beginning of her senior year, she dropped out of Hollywood High School. "Previously I had been a straight-A student," she asserted. "But for some reason I could no longer understand what my teachers were talking about. I could not understand algebra, and I did not understand what 'theme' meant when applied to a novel. History was so boring I could not bear to open my book. I would sit for two hours at the table with my books in front of me, but I could not open them."

Kadohata dropped out of high school in 1973. She got a job as a waitress, clerked at a department store, and worked at a fast-food restaurant. She also sought out her local library. "Seeking it out was more of an instinct, really, not a conscious thought," she said in her Newbery acceptance speech. "I didn't think to myself, 'I need to start reading again.' I felt it. I rediscovered reading—the way I'd read as a child, when there was constantly a book I was just finishing or just beginning or in the middle of. I rediscovered myself." Today libraries hold a special place in her heart. "I look back on 1973, the year I dropped out of school, with the belief that libraries can not just change your life but save it," she acknowledged. "Not the same way a Coast Guardsman or a police officer might save a life, not all at once. It happens more slowly, but just as surely."

She also wrote her first short story. "When I was 17, I wrote the most idiotic story in the world," she recalled in an interview. "It was about all these ducks that had only one leg. They lived on another planet and were a metaphor for humans. I actually sent that story to the *Atlantic Monthly* and, of course, immediately got a rejection. I don't think I wrote anything again until I was in college, when I wrote for the school newspaper." When she was 18, she was admitted to Los Angeles City College. She eventually transferred to University of Southern California, where she graduated with a Bachelor of Arts (BA) degree in journalism in 1977.

"Previously I had been a straight-A student," Kadohata said about changing high schools. "But for some reason I could no longer understand what my teachers were talking about. I could not understand algebra, and I did not understand what 'theme' meant when applied to a novel. History was so boring I could not bear to open my book. I would sit for two hours at the table with my books in front of me, but I could not open them."

That same year Kadohata was injured in a freak auto accident. While she was walking down the street in Los Angeles, a car jumped the curb and hit her. She broke her collarbone and severely mangled her right arm. A doctor told her that if she had come to the hospital any later, she might have had her arm amputated. After several weeks of recovery, she took a month-long trip through parts of America on a Greyhound bus, hoping to find creative inspiration. "I think I felt I needed to conjure up some spirits," she recalled. During that trip, she met several fascinating people and began to rediscover her appreciation of America. It also awakened in her a sense of what it meant to be an American writer. "It did not mean shared history or even shared values with other Americans, but a shared landscape," she contended. "What all of us shared were the factories, the deserts, the cities, the wheat fields. That sharing was an immense responsibility we had to one another. I understood then that I could write about my section of that shared landscape."

Shortly after her travels, Kadohata moved to Boston to live with her sister. She frequented the city's bookstores and began to realize the potential of

Kadohata with her dog, a Doberman named Shika Kojika.

good fiction. "I started looking at short stories," she recalls. "I had always thought that nonfiction represented the 'truth.' Fiction seemed like something that people had done a long time ago, and wasn't very profound. But in these short stories I saw that people were writing now, and that the work was very alive. I realized that you could say things with fiction that you couldn't say any other way."

Becoming a Writer

Determined to become a writer, Kadohata started sending stories to the *Atlantic Monthly* and the *New Yorker* at the rate of one a month. "I wrote 20 to 40 stories, and I got rejections for all of them," she recounts. "But I got letters back that were encouraging, so I kept writing. I remember in 1986, right before I sold my first story to the *New Yorker*, I told a friend that I didn't think I was ever going to sell a story; I wondered if I should stop writing. About three weeks later, I got a phone call from an editor at the *New Yorker.*" After 25 rejections, the magazine had accepted one of her stories, entitled "Charlie O," for publication, and in the coming months they published two more of her stories. Her fiction also appeared in *Grand Street* and the *Pennsylvania Review*.

Kadohata was accepted into the graduate writing program at the University of Pittsburgh. But she felt torn between formal university classes and the education offered through traveling and everyday life. "It's always a battle in my head: 'Oh, I've got to be reading. I feel so guilty,'" she noted. "On the other hand, I feel if I don't go out there and do wacky things, like traveling, it will make my writing dry. Besides, you can't help admiring people who never went to school, travel around, and are incredible writers. There's something romantic about it."

Although she enjoyed her short stint at the University of Pittsburgh, Kadohata wanted to live in New York City. In 1987 she transferred to the graduate writing program at Columbia University. After several months, however, she realized that Columbia's writing program was not helping her. "I went there and I still didn't feel I was getting better, faster," she stated, "so I said, 'Forget it. In the old days they used to say that a young writer has to live in New York to establish a career, but you don't have to anymore.' I had read that somewhere and I said, 'I'm leaving.'" She dropped out of Columbia University in 1988 and committed to becoming a full-time writer.

Kadohata felt torn between formal university classes and the education offered through traveling and everyday life. "It's always a battle in my head: 'Oh, I've got to be reading. I feel so guilty,'" she noted. "On the other hand, I feel if I don't go out there and do wacky things, like traveling, it will make my writing dry. Besides, you can't help admiring people who never went to school, travel around, and are incredible writers. There's something romantic about it."

CAREER HIGHLIGHTS

In late 1987, while on a plane, Kadohata read a profile about successful literary agent Andrew Wylie. When she arrived home to New York, she found two letters from him in her mailbox. He had read her story "Jack's Girl" in the *New Yorker* and was interested in representing her. She was thrilled, and after signing with him she worked to convert the stories she had written into a novel. When she was finished, Wylie took the manuscript, entitled *The Floating World,* and showed it to publishing companies. In the spring of 1988, Viking informed her that they were going to publish her novel.

Even after her first book was accepted for publication, Kadohata did not really think of herself as a writer. "I would go into bookstores and browse through all those how-to-write books," she admitted in an interview. "It still doesn't feel totally natural to say that I'm a writer. I'm still really drawn to that section in a bookstore, and it's still discouraging. It's sort of like picking at a scab." Despite her doubts about herself, however, she did not want to stop writing. "It seems like I had a hunger inside and the only way to feed it was to write," she said.

Writing Novels for Adults

Kadohata's first novel, *The Floating World* (1989), is a coming-of-age tale narrated by 12-year-old Olivia, a young Japanese-American girl growing up in the 1950s. Her father is constantly searching for a job, so Olivia's family moves from town to town, living in what her grandmother Obasan calls "the floating world." Olivia is torn between her Japanese heritage, represented by Obasan, and her American identity, which is encouraged by her parents, who are eager to assimilate into modern America. *The Floating World* received glowing reviews from critics, and Kadohata was praised as a noteworthy new voice in Japanese-American fiction. She had mixed feelings about that. "For the first time in my life, I saw that there could be expectations of me not only as a writer but as an Asian-American writer," she said in *Publishers Weekly*. "On the one hand, I felt like, 'leave me alone.' On the other hand, I thought, 'This is a way I can assert my Asianness.' I wrote the book, and I'm Asian, and I'm the only person who could have written it."

Around the time that *The Floating World* was published, Kadohata moved back to Los Angeles. She quickly fell in love with the city. "At its best, L.A. has a bizarre serenity," she asserted. "When I first moved out here, I remember feeling really disappointed over things, and yet now when I look at the city, I just think it's beautiful. I'm enamored of the city now."

Kadohata's second novel, *In the Heart of the Valley* (1992), did not fare as well with critics or readers. Set in Los Angeles in 2052, it tells the story of a 19-year-old woman named Francie as she struggles to survive in a world that has fallen into lawlessness and chaos. Kadohata had always wanted to write science fiction. "There is something in futuristic fiction that warns, and yet something in it that's very hopeful," she said. "And you can express paranoia in a way that you can't quite do in the present. I like the idea that the author is creating a world that doesn't exist, rather than documenting one that does." Critics, however, found the novel to be unconvincing and ultimately disappointing.

Kadohata's third novel, *The Glass Mountains* (1995), did not receive any significant critical attention. In the story, a young girl's fairy-tale life is torn apart by violence, and she is forced to take drastic action to save her par-

Kadohata's first book for young adults, Kira-Kira, *won the Newbery Medal.*

ents and her village. With the failure of *The Glass Mountains,* Kadohata explored other ways to express herself. In the late 1990s she tried her hand at writing screenplays and worked as a secretary in a food-processing plant.

Becoming a Young Adult Writer

With the advice of a friend, Kadohata soon changed her approach to writing. Caitlyn Dlouhy, an old friend and an editor at Atheneum Books for Young Readers, encouraged her to write a book for young adults. Preoccupied with other projects, Kadohata resisted at first. But when Dlouhy sent boxes of young adult books for her to read, Kadohata began to realize the potential and challenge of young adult fiction. "My previous novels were from the POV [point of view] of young narrators, so the jump from adult books to children's books wasn't extreme," she explained. She was also inspired to write about her childhood. "I guess my childhood is something that has inspired me to do a lot of my writing," she continued. "It's funny, because while I was living my childhood I never dreamed that any of it was future writing material. But I think all of us, no matter what we do and where we live, have fascinating childhoods. So there is always something to write about."

"I guess my childhood is something that has inspired me to do a lot of my writing," Kadohata said. "It's funny, because while I was living my childhood I never dreamed that any of it was future writing material. But I think all of us, no matter what we do and where we live, have fascinating childhoods. So there is always something to write about."

Kadohata's first young adult book, *Kira-Kira,* tells the story of two young Japanese-American sisters, Lynn and Katie, growing up in Georgia in the 1950s. Katie, the novel's narrator, idolizes her strong older sister, who taught her the meaning of "kira-kira," which is the Japanese word for "glittering." The family faces prejudice and discrimination as well as economic and emotional hardships, which are compounded when Lynn becomes ill. During this difficult time, Katie comes to appreciate small moments with her sister and her family and struggles to keep her joy of life despite her sister's illness. According to Kadohata, "the message behind *Kira-Kira* is that life is complicated, but wonderful, and you should never lose the ability to feel wonder over even the smallest thing."

Kira-Kira was a huge success with critics and readers. Reviewers praised Kadohata's lyrical prose and insightful descriptions of people in the book. They believed that the novel really expressed the challenges of growing up as a Japanese-American in the 1950s as well as the experience of illness and loss. Kadohata was awarded the prestigious Newbery Medal for *Kira-Kira,* which is an impressive achievement for a first-time young adult author. Receiving the award was an amazing experience for her. "It was shocking and purely joyful," she exulted. "I've never experienced a feeling like it. The joy was just so incredibly intense. One analogy I can think of is that it was like in Chicago when we would go to Lake Michigan on windy days and the waves would hit us so hard we would fall over and even get bruised. And yet it was so much fun. The feeling when the waves hit you was thrilling and yet also a strong physical feeling."

In her next book, *Weedflower* (2006), Kadohata focused on the experiences of Japanese-Americans uprooted from their lives and moved to internment camps during World War II. In the book, a young Japanese girl, Sumiko, forms an unlikely friendship with a Mohave boy. Reviewers praised her vivid descriptions of life in the camp and the compelling character portrayals in the novel, as in this comment from *Publishers Weekly*: "Kadohata clearly and eloquently conveys her heroine's mixture of shame, anger, and courage. Readers will be inspired."

Kadohata was moved to write about this dark time in American history by her father's experiences. "My father was interned in that camp," she revealed. "The other reason has to do with my belief that it is not just the sharing of values but the sharing of this amazing land that makes us Americans. So I wanted to write about how two groups of people sharing a land can change the world."

ADVICE TO YOUNG WRITERS

Kadohata has advised young writers to keep at it, because writing is a difficult profession. "Persevere," she cautioned. "If your parents are smart they will tell you not to be a writer. You have to be 100 percent certain that you want to do it." She has described her own creative process as writing everything and then going back and editing later. "I had read a long time ago that the best way to write is make a mess and then clean it up. I've read that some writers write each sentence over and over until it's perfect and then move on to the next sentence. [But] I try to get everything down as quickly as possible. Then I have a tremendous mess and I clean it up and think it's wonderful. Then my editor tells me to rewrite it!"

MARRIAGE AND FAMILY

Kadohata has been married once. She and her husband divorced in 2000, but she doesn't talk much about it. Today she has a serious boyfriend whom she describes as a great supporter of her writing. She lives in Long Beach, California, with her son, Samuel Bahytzhan Kadohata, whom she adopted in 2004 from Kazakhstan (part of the former Soviet Union). She also has a dog, a Doberman named Shika Kojika that she adoped from a dog rescue service.

HOBBIES AND OTHER INTERESTS

Traveling is one of Kadohata's favorite hobbies. "I'm a road hog!" she claimed. "I love to travel around this amazing country. The beautiful landscape, the highways—I love it. Traveling, seeing the country, is one of the things from which I derive my 'writing energy.' Just thinking about the American landscape and focusing on it puts me in touch with what I think of as the real, essential me. I have to be in touch with this real, essential me whenever I sit down to write."

WRITINGS

Novels for Young Adults

Kira-Kira, 2004
Weedflower, 2006

Novels for Adults

The Floating World, 1989
In the Heart of the Valley of Love, 1992
The Glass Mountains, 1995

HONORS AND AWARDS

National Endowment for the Arts Fellowship: 1991
Whiting Writers Award (Whiting Foundation): 1991
Newbery Medal (American Library Association): 2005, for *Kira-Kira*

FURTHER READING

Periodicals

Horn Book Magazine, Mar.-Apr. 2004, p.183; July-Aug. 2005, p.419
Los Angeles Times, Apr. 30, 2006, p.10
Publishers Weekly, Aug. 3, 1992, p.48
School Library Journal, May 2005, p.38
Washington Post, Jan. 31, 2005, p.C12

Online Articles

http://cynthialeitichsmith.blogspot.com/2006/02/author-feature-cynthia-kadohata.html
(Cynastations, "Author Feature: Cynthia Kadohata," Feb. 20, 2006)
http://www.lili.org/read/letstalk/themes-books/otherrev.htm#kadohata
(Other Americas Author Information and Book Reviews, Idaho Commission for Libraries, "Cynthia Kadohata," June 6, 2006)
http://www.timeforkids.com/TFK/kidscoops/story/0,14989,1028042,00.html
(Time for Kids, "TFK Talks with Cynthia Kadohata," Feb. 28, 2005)

Online Databases

Biography Resource Center Online, 2006, articles from *Contemporary Authors Online,* 2006, and *Notable Asian Americans,* 2006

ADDRESS

Cynthia Kadohata
Simon & Schuster
1230 Avenue of the Americas
New York, NY 10020

WORLD WIDE WEB SITE

http://www.kira-kira.us

Coretta Scott King 1927-2006

American Civil Rights Activist, Writer, and Speaker
Widow of Slain Civil Rights Leader Dr. Martin Luther King Jr. and Founder of The King Center

BIRTH

Coretta Scott King was born Coretta Scott on April 27, 1927, in Heiberger, Alabama. She was the second of three children born to Obadiah "Obie" Scott, a truck driver and grocery store owner, and Bernice (McMurry) Scott, a homemaker. She had an older sister, Edythe, and a younger brother, Obie.

YOUTH

Although they were not rich, Coretta Scott King's family was considered fairly well off by standards of the time for African Americans. They lived in a two-room house in Perry County near Marion, Alabama, on land that had been owned by the Scott family for three generations, since slavery was abolished at the end of the Civil War. African-American landowners were rare in the southern United States at that time.

King's father, Obie Scott, worked a variety of jobs to provide for the family. He was the first African American in the area to own a truck, and he used it to haul logs and pulp wood for the local timber companies and saw mills. At various times he was also a barber, a taxi driver, and a farmer, and he briefly owned his own sawmill. He made enough of an income that Coretta's mother did not have to work. This was unusual at the time. The United States was in the midst of the Great Depression, and poverty was widespread. Most people—black and white—struggled just to get by.

To earn spending money for movies and other treats, King sometimes picked cotton on neighbors' farms. She wrote in her autobiography, "If you made four or five dollars in the course of a season, that was pretty good money in those Depression days. I remember one special year when I made seven dollars picking cotton. I was always very strong, and I made a very good cotton picker." She enjoyed being outdoors, running and playing games. She was also a tomboy who often got into fights with her brother.

In 1937, when Coretta was ten years old, the Scott family left their farmhouse and moved to a larger house. They rented the new house to be closer to town and the children's school. Her father continued to operate his trucking business and he also opened a small grocery store in town.

Experiencing Segregation and Racism

King grew up in a time of widespread legal discrimination against African Americans. Racial segregation was enforced throughout the southern United States by "Jim Crow" laws. This meant that African Americans and whites had "separate but equal" public facilities—housing, schools, bathrooms, drinking fountains, seating in movie theaters and on buses, and more. Although these separate facilities were called equal, in reality the facilities provided for whites were far superior to those provided for African Americans.

Segregation was such a part of everyday life that African Americans were not allowed to sit in an ice cream parlor or drink from a glass in a restau-

King grew up at a time when segregation was widespread in the American south, as in this 1938 photo of a "colored" drinking fountain at a county courthouse.

rant. They could not vote or serve on a courtroom jury. They were treated as inferior, and they were expected to act subservient to whites. In many places, blacks were required to step aside to allow whites to pass by on the sidewalks. "As an African American growing up in the segregated south, I was told, one way or another, almost every day of my life, that I wasn't as good as a white child," King recalled. "When I went to the movies with other black children, we had to sit in the balcony while the white kids got to sit in the better seats below. We had to walk to school while the white children rode in school buses paid for by our parents' taxes. Such messages, saying we were inferior, were a daily part of our lives."

The "Jim Crow" laws made it very dangerous for African Americans to disobey the rules of segregation. Punishments ranged from harassment to being put in jail, and sometime even lynching—murder by a mob without a trial or legal protection. Because her father's business ventures were in direct competition with white men doing the same type of work, he was often subjected to threats and intimidation. The family's rented house burned down, as did his sawmill after being in business for only two weeks. There were rumors that the fires had been purposely set by local white supremacists who wanted to scare King's father so that he would stop taking away their business. Nothing came of these suspicions and the fires remained a mystery that was never investigated.

Obie Scott responded to the destruction of his family's rented home by building a much larger, nicer three-bedroom house in town. The new house was located next to the grocery store he owned and near the African Methodist Episcopal Zion Church attended by the family. Coretta's parents encouraged their children to rise above their circumstances and not to give in to those who wanted to see them fail. Coretta explained, "I had wonderful parents who inspired me to be the best person that I could be, and my mother always told me that I was going to go to college, even if she didn't have but one dress to put on. So I grew up knowing that I was going to somehow find a way out of the situation I grew up in."

“

"As an African American growing up in the segregated south, I was told, one way or another, almost every day of my life, that I wasn't as good as a white child," Coretta recalled. *"When I went to the movies with other black children, we had to sit in the balcony while the white kids got to sit in the better seats below. We had to walk to school while the white children rode in school buses paid for by our parents' taxes. Such messages, saying we were inferior, were a daily part of our lives."*

”

EDUCATION

King began her education at the Crossroads School in Marion, Alabama. She walked five miles every day to get to the one-room school for African-American children. Every day she was passed by a school bus carrying white children to their school. The white school was closer than Crossroads, but segregation laws prevented her from enrolling there. She thought about this every day as the school bus passed her by. Later in her life, she remembered this as the very beginning of her realization that society needed to change.

After graduating from Crossroads at the top of her class, King attended the private Lincoln High School in Marion. The school was ten miles away, so students normally had to stay in town for the school week, only going home on the weekends. Her mother, Bernice Scott, thought that the children should not have to be away from home for that long, so she decided to find a way to allow them to come home every day. She located a bus and she drove the children back and forth to school every day herself. During that time, this was an extremely unusual thing for a woman to do. Most women didn't drive at all, and if they did, they certainly didn't drive buses.

Lincoln High was an unusual school for that time and place. It was a high school for African-American students, and all of the students were black. But the teaching staff was integrated, with both black and white teachers. Perhaps most shocking at the time, teachers of both races lived together in dormitories. Despite this unconventional arrangement, there were no reported racial incidents directed at the school. The school was progressive, encouraging independent thinking as well as academic excellence. It was the first time King had known any college-educated people, and she quickly began to thrive as a student. She was interested in philosophy and began to form her own ideas about the social changes that she thought were needed. She also developed a keen interest in music, learning to play the trumpet and the piano and discovering a talent for singing. She graduated as valedictorian of her class in 1945.

"

"I had wonderful parents who inspired me to be the best person that I could be, and my mother always told me that I was going to go to college, even if she didn't have but one dress to put on. So I grew up knowing that I was going to somehow find a way out of the situation I grew up in."

Going to College

After high school, King enrolled in Antioch College, a progressive, integrated school in Yellow Springs, Ohio. Although she was awarded a scholarship, she was initially hesitant about studying at Antioch. She knew that northern schools were generally better than schools in the south, and also that at that time there weren't any colleges in Alabama that would accept African-American students. Antioch College was her best opportunity to continue her education. Even so, she was worried about having to compete with white students who were much better prepared for higher education, having attended better elementary and high schools than those available to African Americans. She went to Antioch in spite of her worries, and later said that it was there that she learned how to live in a white community.

Antioch was known for its emphasis on training students to create social change. King credits the college with preparing her for the role she would play later in life. She became very politically aware at Antioch and began her career as an activist. She joined the local chapter of the National Association for the Advancement of Colored People (NAACP) in its very early days and was also a member of the college's Race Relations and Civil

An enlarged secton of a class photo from Antioch College, November 1945. King is marked #355.

Liberties Committees. In 1948, she was named a delegate to the founding convention of the Young Progressives organization.

The college's mandatory work-study program was another unique aspect of the Antioch educational approach. As one of the students who pioneered the new program, King was required to alternate semesters of study with time spent working at a job. She felt that her classes were more meaningful because of this, as working helped her apply what she was learning in the classroom to a real situation. During her working semesters, she had jobs as a waitress, a camp counselor, a library assistant, and a nursery school attendant. Sometimes she worked in her father's store as a bookkeeper, and she also ordered the store's supplies and waited on customers. These seemingly odd jobs were all credited as part of the college's work-study program.

Planning a Career in Music

King also continued her music studies at Antioch. She sang in the choir and was a soloist with the Second Baptist Church in Springfield, Ohio. In 1948 she gave her first singing concert. She decided to pursue a degree in music and elementary education, thinking that she would have a career teaching and singing in concerts. But when it came time to perform her student teaching, she discovered that none of the schools in the area would accept an African-American teacher. She had no option other than to take a student teaching position at the Antioch Demonstration School, which was operated by the College.

This was a great disappointment to King and caused her to rethink her plan to work as a teacher. She was angry and frustrated, and thought about how she had come to Ohio from Alabama specifically to escape segregation. She later recalled telling herself, "I have to face these problems. So I'm not going to let this one get me down. I'll have to accept a compromise now, but I don't have to accept it as being right. I'm going to do something about this situation. I don't want those who come after me to have to experience the same fate I did." She graduated from Antioch in 1951 with a Bachelor of Arts (BA) degree in music and education, a new plan to continue her music studies, and a resolve to work for social change.

King applied for and received a scholarship to the New England Conservatory of Music in Boston, Massachusetts. The scholarship paid for her tuition, but she was responsible for all her other expenses. She worked part-time as a mail order clerk and also cleaned house for a Boston family in exchange for a room and breakfast each day. With hardly any money left over to buy food, she existed as best she could on a diet consisting mainly of crackers, peanut butter, and fruit. After her first year at the Conservatory, King began to receive financial aid from the State of Alabama, under a program that assisted African-American students who were not allowed to enroll in the state's colleges. Things were a little better for her with the increased financial support, and she was able to focus more fully on her studies.

A Fateful Meeting

While she was studying at the New England Conservatory, a mutual friend introduced Coretta to Martin Luther King Jr. After a short telephone conversation, she agreed to meet him for lunch. When they met for the first time in person, she remembered being very unimpressed. She thought he was too short, and she was put off by his plans to become a Baptist minister. However, as they got to know each other over lunch, she began to change her mind. She realized that he was not the stereotyped preacher that she had imagined. "In those few minutes I had forgotten about Martin being short and had completely revised my first impression. He radiated charm. When he talked, he grew in stature. . . . I knew immediately that he was special," she recalled. But when he told her at the end of that first date that he wanted to marry her, she replied, "That's absurd. You don't even know me." She later reflected that he seemed very certain of what he was proposing. "It was as if he had no time for mistakes, as if he had to make up his mind quickly and correctly, and then move on with his life."

After they had dated for awhile, Martin again asked her to marry him. Coretta took six months to think it over before she said yes. Although she felt that marrying him would mean giving up her wish for a career as a singer, she realized that they shared similar goals in life. They both wanted very much to bring about social changes for the benefit of African Americans. Writing in her autobiography, Coretta recalled, "I had a strong faith. I always believed that there was a purpose for my life, and that I had to seek that purpose, and that if I discovered that purpose, then I believed that I would be successful in what I was doing. And I thought I had found that purpose when I decided that music was going to be my career—concert singing. . . . After I met Martin and prayed about whether or not I should open myself to that relationship, I had a dream, and in that dream, I was made to feel that I should allow myself to be open and stop fighting the relationship. And that's what I did, and of course the rest is history."

“

"I had a strong faith. I always believed that there was a purpose for my life, and that I had to seek that purpose. . . . After I met Martin and prayed about whether or not I should open myself to that relationship, I had a dream, and in that dream, I was made to feel that I should allow myself to be open and stop fighting the relationship. And that's what I did, and of course the rest is history."

Getting Married

Coretta Scott married Martin Luther King Jr. on June 18, 1953, in the garden of her parents' home in Marion, Alabama. The wedding ceremony was performed by Martin Luther King Sr., who reluctantly agreed to Coretta's unconventional refusal to include the bride's traditional vows to obey her husband. The wedding was the largest event the town had ever seen, with 350 guests representing a combination of big city visitors from Atlanta and local residents and farmers. Because all the hotels near Marion were whites-only and would not rent rooms to African Americans, the newlyweds spent their wedding night at the home of the local undertaker.

King and her husband, Martin Luther King, with three of their four children at their home in Atlanta, Georgia, March 1963. From left: Martin Luther III, age five; Dexter Scott, age two, and Yolanda Denise, age seven. Their youngest daughter, Bernice Albertine, was not yet born at the time of this photo.

After the wedding, the couple returned to Boston and lived there while Coretta finished her studies. She earned her second Bachelor of Arts (BA) degree in voice and violin from the New England Conservatory in 1954. They moved to Montgomery, Alabama, in September 1954. They eventually had four children: Yolanda Denise King, Martin Luther King III, Dexter Scott King, and Rev. Bernice Albertine King.

CAREER HIGHLIGHTS

Challenging Segregation

During the mid-1950s, people all over the south were beginning to challenge segregation. African Americans had already been organizing in groups to protest segregation in transportation and schools. Then on December 1, 1955, in Montgomery, Alabama, Rosa Parks refused to give up her seat on a city bus to a white passenger. (For more information on Parks, see *Biography Today,* April 2006.) Parks was arrested and put on trial for causing a public disturbance and violating segregation laws, sparking a call for a city-wide boycott of the transportation system. When Martin was chosen to lead the Montgomery Bus Boycott, Coretta's life changed forever. She was no longer simply the wife of a southern Baptist preacher—she was becoming the wife of a civil rights pioneer.

> *"My wife was always stronger than I was through the struggle," Martin Luther King wrote. "I am convinced that if I had not had a wife with the fortitude, strength, and calmness of Coretta, I could not have stood up amid the ordeals and tensions surrounding the Montgomery movement. . . . In the darkest moments she always brought the light of hope."*

The Montgomery Bus Boycott and the ensuing legal battles lasted just over a year. The boycott still stands as one of the largest and most successful nonviolent protests against racial segregation ever held. Martin's role in leading and organizing the boycott resulted in hundreds of death threats and threats of violence against his family. In January 1956, just a month after the Montgomery bus system was integrated, several anonymous telephone calls came to the King family home. Callers threatened to bomb the house if Martin didn't leave town within three days. He ignored the threats. Three days later, on January 30, 1956, Coretta was at home with her infant daughter and a friend. A bomb thrown at the house blew up the front porch, with Coretta, her friend, and the baby barely escaping harm. Coretta said that from that day on, she knew that her family would always be in danger.

Despite the ongoing threats and her deepening involvement in civil rights activism, Coretta remained committed to her husband's mission. Martin wrote in his autobiography, "My wife was always stronger than I was through the struggle. I am convinced that if I had not had a wife with the fortitude, strength, and calmness of Coretta, I could not have stood up amid the ordeals and tensions surrounding the Montgomery movement. I came to see the real meaning of that rather trite statement: 'A wife can either make or break a husband.' Coretta proved to be that type of wife with qualities to make a husband when he could have been so easily broken. In the darkest moments she always brought the light of hope."

As her husband began to travel extensively to organize and support protests across the country, Coretta stayed home to handle administrative duties of the civil rights movement while raising four children. She sometimes traveled with him, most notably on a 1957 trip to Ghana and a month-long tour of India in 1959. By 1960, the family had moved to Atlanta, Georgia. Martin was one of the most recognized leaders in the civil rights movement, and Coretta was gaining a reputation as an activist in her own right.

Working as an Activist

Coretta was a dedicated assistant in her husband's civil rights work, but she also made her own contributions to the movement. In 1962 she served as a Women's Strike for Peace delegate to the Disarmament Conference held in Geneva, Switzerland, and attended by representatives of 17 nations. Coretta taught voice in the music department of the Morris Brown College in Atlanta, and also used her musical talents to advance civil rights. She created and performed several critically acclaimed Freedom Concerts, blending music, spoken word narration, and poetry to portray important events in the civil rights movement. She used these performances to raise money for her husband's Southern Christian Leadership Conference (SCLC), an organization he helped to found to promote nonviolent social activism. In 1965, Coretta accompanied her husband on the famous march from Selma, Alabama, to Montgomery, Alabama.

The march had started as a peaceful event. But when protesters tried to cross the Edmund Pettus Bridge, which led into Selma, they were met by Alabama state troopers. The troopers began a violent assault on the protestors, which was documented by reporters. The attack in Selma quickly came to be known as "Bloody Sunday." The police response was so terrible and vicious that it horrified the nation. Within the next few days, demonstrations in support of the marchers were held in 80 cities. Thousands of religious and lay leaders, including Coretta and Martin Luther King, flew to Selma. Outraged citizens flooded the White House and Congress with letters and phone calls. Bloody Sunday convinced President Lyndon B.

Coretta and Martin lead the final lap of the Selma to Montgomery march demanding voter registration rights for blacks, March 1965.

Johnson to send new voting-rights legislation to Congress. On August 6, 1965, Johnson signed the Voting Rights Act into law. It ended literacy tests and poll taxes and ordered the appointment of federal voting registrars who would ensure the rights of black voters, resulting in a dramatic increase in the number of African Americans who were able to vote. It has been called the single most effective piece of civil rights legislation ever passed by the United States Congress.

Meanwhile, amidst impressive progress towards real social change, Martin continued to receive death threats. When the threatening anonymous telephone calls came, Coretta sometimes responded by informing the caller that her husband was busy and did not wish to be disturbed. She would say, "He told me to write the name and number of anyone who called to threaten his life so that he could return the call later." Not surprisingly, no one ever provided her with that information. But responding in this way projected the attitude of quiet confidence that came to characterize Coretta's personality.

The Assassination

On April 4, 1968, Coretta went on a shopping trip with her youngest daughter Yolanda. They were buying new dresses to wear for Easter. When they returned home, Coretta received a telephone call from Rev. Jesse Jackson, telling her that her husband had been shot. Martin Luther

King Jr. had been assassinated in Memphis, Tennessee, where he had gone to lead a protest march. "It hit me hard," Coretta said, "that the call I seemed subconsciously to have been waiting for all our lives had come." She recalled that when President John F. Kennedy had been shot and killed in 1963, Martin told her, "That's exactly what's going to happen to me."

In the days immediately following the assassination, race riots erupted in cities across the country. Coretta spoke out to ask for a restoration of peace, and is credited with helping to subdue the violence before it became too severe. 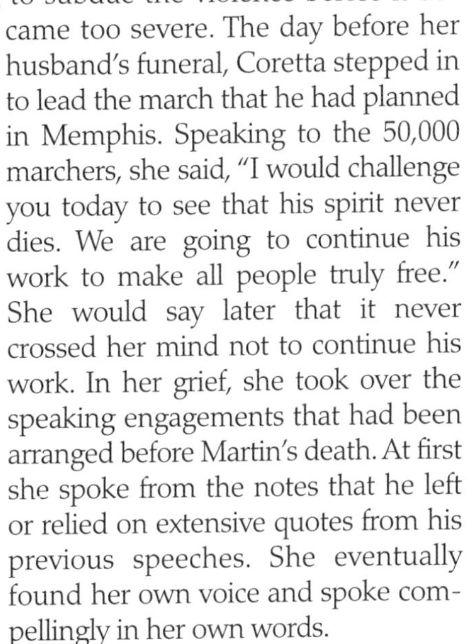The day before her husband's funeral, Coretta stepped in to lead the march that he had planned in Memphis. Speaking to the 50,000 marchers, she said, "I would challenge you today to see that his spirit never dies. We are going to continue his work to make all people truly free." She would say later that it never crossed her mind not to continue his work. In her grief, she took over the speaking engagements that had been arranged before Martin's death. At first she spoke from the notes that he left or relied on extensive quotes from his previous speeches. She eventually found her own voice and spoke compellingly in her own words.

"

The day before her husband's funeral, Coretta stepped in to lead the march that he had planned in Memphis. Speaking to the 50,000 marchers, she said, "I would challenge you today to see that his spirit never dies. We are going to continue his work to make all people truly free."

"

On June 26, 1968, just a few months after her husband's death, Coretta founded the nonprofit Martin Luther King Jr. Center for Nonviolent Social Change, later known as the King Center. Originally, she ran the group from of her home in Atlanta, Georgia. Her goal was to carry on Martin's philosophy of nonviolent resistance. The Center was intended to establish a living memorial to Dr. King, to preserve his papers, and to promote his teachings. At the same time, Coretta also formed a committee to work towards the establishment of a national holiday in his honor. Determined to make both the Center and the holiday a reality, she would spend the next 15 years in pursuit of that goal.

In 1969 Coretta published her autobiography, titled *My Life with Martin Luther King, Jr.* The book is a personal account of the unfolding civil rights movement as she witnessed it, including glimpses of their private life.

Although the book has been criticized for providing an incomplete, uncritical picture of the civil rights leader, it has also been praised as a warm and human recounting of events. Ultimately, it is seen as a personal portrait of Martin as only his wife could provide.

Fighting Racial Discrimination

In the years after the assassination of her husband, Coretta Scott King dedicated herself to continuing his unfinished work. She made it her life's mission to promote his philosophy of nonviolent social action and to continue to speak about his ideals. She became a talented, respected speaker who was widely admired and much in demand. She brought attention to human rights issues and began to speak out against racial discrimination—not only in the United States, but all over the world. King visited many countries to bring her husband's message of using nonviolence and peaceful resistance to create social changes. On March 17, 1969, she became the first woman to ever make a speech in the historic St. Paul's Cathedral in London, England.

———— “ ————

"I had a commitment even before I met Martin. If I didn't believe in this, I wouldn't be working 18-hour days. I don't have another life. This is my life. . . . I didn't learn my commitment from Martin. We just converged at a certain time."

King was soon recognized as an influential civil rights leader. She received several awards from international organizations honoring her humanitarian efforts and dedication to civil rights for all people. In 1968 she was named Woman of the Year by the National Association of Television and Radio Announcers. And in 1969, the American Library Association gave its first annual Coretta Scott King Award to honor authors and illustrators who have promoted the vision of Martin Luther King Jr. The award, which is still given today, focuses specifically on works that may have been overlooked because of conscious or unconscious racism.

Throughout the 1970s King used her speaking engagements to tirelessly promote the dream of creating what her husband called a "beloved community," a world in which all people were treated with equal dignity and given equal opportunities to succeed. In January 1975, a Good Housekeeping magazine poll named Coretta Scott King as one of the 40 most respected women in the United States. She also received several honorary doctorate degrees from colleges and universities all over the country. But it was in the 1980s that her dedication and hard work was rewarded as she achieved two of her most important goals.

President Reagan at the signing ceremony in the White House Rose Garden for Martin Luther King Day holiday legislation, November 1983.

Two Victories

In 1981, King relocated the operation of the King Center from her home to a brand new facility that opened in Atlanta. The expansive new complex houses several exhibit areas documenting the civil rights movement, a 250-seat auditorium for presentations and speeches, an extensive library and archive Martin Luther King's papers and writings, and his gravesite. Millions of people visit the Center each year to pay their respects to his memory, learn about the civil rights movement, study his work, and be trained to organize nonviolent protests. Since its formation, the King Center has trained tens of thousands of activists from all over the world in the philosophy and practice of nonviolence.

Then within two years of the King Center's grand opening, on November 2, 1983, President Ronald Reagan signed legislation designating the third Monday in January as a federal holiday honoring Martin Luther King Jr. Finally, 15 years of organizing, educating, petitioning, and political lobbying had paid off. Although it was another two years before the Martin Luther King Jr. holiday was observed for the first time on January 20, 1986, Coretta Scott King's success was not diminished by the delay. Clayborne Carson, director of the King Papers Project at Stanford University told the *Atlanta Journal-Constitution,* "I don't think people give her enough credit

Coretta Scott King continued her work as an activist on behalf of human rights throughout her life. She is shown here protesting apartheid in South Africa outside the embassy in Washington DC, November 1984.

for doing something very few people have done. If she hadn't been as dedicated and energetic as she was, the King Center wouldn't exist and the King holiday wouldn't exist."

Coretta intended the King holiday to be more than just another day off from work or school. She wanted people to use the day as an opportunity to reflect on the life and teachings of Martin Luther King Jr., and to find ways to build the "beloved community." This dream could be realized only by people working together to create necessary changes. "We have called for people to remember to celebrate, and most importantly, to act," she declared. "We like to say we celebrate the birthday and not memorialize it, as we do in April. Now we should ask people to really commemorate his life with some form of service and to give back to the community."

A Global Perspective

Even after achieving her dream of opening the King Center and creating a national King holiday, Coretta Scott King did not stop working to advance the worldwide cause of civil and human rights. In 1983 she organized the Coalition of Conscience to sponsor the 20th Anniversary March on Washington, commemorating the 1963 event at which Martin Luther King delivered his historic "I Have a Dream" speech. In 1985, Coretta and three of her children were arrested for protesting South Africa's apartheid system of racial segregation and discrimination. In 1988 she reconvened the Coalition of Conscience and led more than 55,000 people in the 25th Anniversary March on Washington. In 1988 she also served as the head of the U.S. delegation of Women for a Meaningful Summit in Athens, Greece, and in 1990 she was a co-organizer of the Soviet-American Women's Summit in Washington.

In reflecting on her life of service to the civil rights movement, Coretta Scott King said, "I had a commitment even before I met Martin. If I didn't believe in this, I wouldn't be working 18-hour days. I don't have another life. This is my life. I'd like to see the legacy [of Martin Luther King] prevail because if it does, we would have a better world.... I didn't learn my commitment from Martin. We just converged at a certain time." She ran the King Center for nearly 30 years, turning the leadership duties over to her son Dexter Scott King in 1995. She briefly resumed her role as the head of the Center in 2004, until her son Martin Luther King III took over as the Center's president later that year.

"She was a freedom fighter. She marched in Birmingham. She marched in Selma. When [Martin Luther King] was killed, she kept marching for workers' rights."
—Rev. Jessie Jackson

”

Later Years

King was a strict vegetarian who began every day with prayer, meditation, and exercise. She eventually adopted a raw-food diet and gained a reputation for drinking lots of oddly colored vegetable juice that she made herself. Her workday usually began at 7:00 a.m. and often lasted until 2:00 a.m. the next day. She was known for conducting most of her business over the telephone as she continued to travel extensively for speaking engagements.

In her later years, King continued to work for social change and world peace. She focused her activism on critical issues and concerns of disadvantaged people all over the world. She was an outspoken advocate for the cancellation of the national debts of African nations, and she brought attention to such global issues as AIDS and worldwide health security, voting rights and individual responsibility, racial justice and race relations, disarmament and peaceful conflict resolution, and reductions in military spending. She spoke out against the death penalty and called for stronger

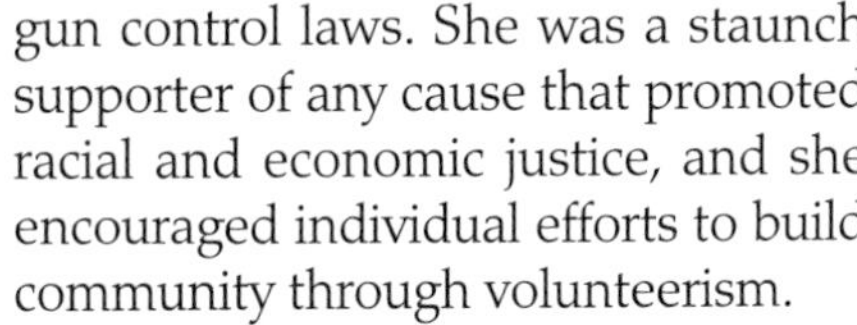

gun control laws. She was a staunch supporter of any cause that promoted racial and economic justice, and she encouraged individual efforts to build community through volunteerism.

> "
>
> *"She was always more of an activist than Martin. Although people didn't realize it, the action part was always difficult for him. He wanted to preach and reason things out. Coretta wanted to march." —Andrew Young*
>
> "

King's strength and energy had been legendary, and even late in her life she was able to maintain a schedule that exhausted many of her younger assistants. But her health declined in 2005 and she suffered a series of heart attacks and strokes. By August 2005, she was severely weakened and unable to speak, although she could still sing. Despite a regimen of speech therapy and physical rehabilitation, she never fully recovered. On January 14, 2006, she made her last public appearance at the King Center's annual Salute to Greatness dinner. On January 26, 2006, she traveled to Mexico to seek treatment at a private hospital in Rosarito Beach, just south of San Diego, California. On January 30, 2006, Coretta Scott King died in her sleep at the hospital. Upon her death it was revealed that she had been battling ovarian cancer and had gone to Mexico for experimental treatment that was unavailable in the United States. The official cause of her death was listed as heart failure and ovarian cancer.

LEGACY

Coretta Scott King's lifelong dedication to advancing civil rights and her many successes in bringing about social change gave her an international reputation as a woman of great influence. She supported nonviolent freedom struggles around the world and served as an advocate for racial equality, economic justice, religious freedom, and dignity and human rights for women and children, gays and lesbians, and people with disabilities. Rev. Jesse Jackson said, "She was a freedom fighter. She marched in Birmingham. She marched in Selma. When [Martin Luther King Jr.] was killed, she kept marching for workers' rights."

King received much public recognition and numerous awards for her work, including honorary doctorate degrees from more than 60 colleges and universities. She wrote or contributed to dozens of books, edited several collections of her late husband's work, and published a nationally syndicated newspaper column. She helped found dozens of organizations including the Black Leadership Forum, the National Black Coalition for Voter Participation, and the Black Leadership Roundtable. She was also a member of the board of directors many organizations, including the National Organization for Women and the Southern Christian Leadership Conference.

King's legacy is as much a reflection of her personal character as it is of her accomplishments. She is remembered for her grace and dignity, her personal strength in times of crisis, and her equal devotion to her family and the civil rights movement. She is a woman who overcame tragedy, held her family together, and became an inspirational presence around the world. Longtime friend Andrew Young said she handled public scrutiny well and never lost her poise or showed anger, even in the face of criticism that was often harsh. Young said in *People,* "She was always more of an activist than Martin. Although people didn't realize it, the action part was always difficult for him. He wanted to preach and reason things out. Coretta wanted to march."

Speaking just after King's death, Rev. Al Sharpton talked about what made her such an effective leader. "She was a mixture of regal bearing and grace and an uncompromising freedom fighter," Rev. Sharpton said. "[People] saw her in her regality and aura and didn't realize that in her heart was a woman who believed what her husband fought for. She didn't walk behind her husband, she walked beside him. . . . She was a real activist. She had one of the most keen, aggressive social political minds that I have ever talked to. She was really committed to world peace, really committed to racial equality, really committed to civil disobedience and nonviolence. She was not just the woman [Martin Luther King Jr.] went home to. She was the one who shaped his ideas and activism and she single-handedly maintained his legacy."

"She didn't walk behind her husband, she walked beside him. . . . She was a real activist. She had one of the most keen, aggressive social political minds that I have ever talked to. . . . She was not just the woman [Martin Luther King Jr.] went home to. She was the one who shaped his ideas and activism and she single-handedly maintained his legacy." —Rev. Al Sharpton

”

Perhaps King's own words describe her legacy best. She wrote in her autobiography, "I believe that there is a plan and a purpose for each person's life and that there are forces working in the universe to bring about good and to create a community of love and brotherhood. . . . I think what I've tried to do is to empower people to understand that they can make a difference. And by using the method of nonviolence as a way of life, it becomes internalized into your life; so everything that you seek to do, you use those principles. . . . I think we have cause for hope, especially if we can rekindle a new era of social activism and voter participation to achieve the reforms needed to produce genuine equality, economic opportunity for all, and peace with justice. If we keep faith with Martin's teachings and join together with an energized recommitment to create the beloved community, we will one day be celebrating his vision as a glorious reality."

"I think what I've tried to do is to empower people to understand that they can make a difference," King explained. "And by using the method of nonviolence as a way of life, it becomes internalized into your life; so everything that you seek to do, you use those principles."

WRITINGS

My Life with Martin Luther King, Jr., 1969
The Words of Martin Luther King, Jr., 1983

HONORS AND AWARDS

Annual Brotherhood Award (National Council on Negro Women): 1957
Distinguished Achievement Award (National Organization of Colored Women's Clubs): 1962
Citation for work in peace and freedom (Women's Strike for Peace): 1963
Louise Waterman Wise Award (American Jewish Congress Women's Authority): 1963
Wateler Peace Prize: 1968
Woman of Conscience Award (National Council of Women): 1968
Woman of the Year (National Association of Television and Radio Announcers): 1968
Dag Hammarskjold Award (World Organization of the Diplomatic Press): 1969
Nehru Award for International Understanding: 1969
Pacem in Terris Award (International Overseas Service Foundation): 1969
Leadership for Freedom Award (Roosevelt University): 1971
Martin Luther King Memorial Medal (College of the City of New York): 1971

Named one of the 40 Most Respected Women in the United States (*Good Housekeeping*): 1975
UAW Social Justice Award (United Auto Workers Union): 1980
Eugene V. Debs Award: 1982
Candace Award (National Coalition of 100 Black Women): 1987
Freedom Award (National Civil Rights Museum): 1991
Frontrunner Award (Sarah Lee Corporation): 1996
Humanitarian Award (Martin Luther King Jr. State Holiday Commission): 1999
Congressional Gold Medal (United States Congress): 2004

FURTHER READING

Books

Contemporary Black Biography, Vol. 3, 1992
Jakoubek, Robert. *Black Americans of Achievement: Martin Luther King, Jr.*, 2005
King, Coretta Scott. *My Life with Martin Luther King, Jr.*, 1969
Notable Black American Women, 1992
Press, Petra. *Coretta Scott King: An Unauthorized Biography*, 2000
Rhodes, Lisa Renee. *Black Americans of Achievement: Coretta Scott King*, 2005
Schraff, Anne. *Coretta Scott King: Striving for Civil Rights*, 1997
Siebold, Thomas. *People Who Made History: Martin Luther King, Jr.*, 2000
Who's Who in America, 2006

Periodicals

Atlanta Journal-Constitution, Feb. 1, 2006, p.A1; Feb. 4, 2006, p.A11; Feb. 7, 2006, pp.A1, D4, D6, D8, D14, and D19; Feb. 8, 2006, pp.A1 and D6
Current Biography Yearbook, 1969
Ebony, Jan. 1990, p.116; Jan. 2002, p.116; Aug. 2003, p.164
New York Times, Feb. 1, 2006, p.A1
People, June 22, 1998, p.46
Times (London), Feb. 1, 2006, p.60
U.S. News & World Report, Jan. 16, 1995, p.54

Online Articles

http://www.stanford.edu/group/King//about_king/encyclopedia/king_coretta_scott.htm
(King Encyclopedia, "King, Coretta Scott (1927-2006)," undated)
http://www.achievement.org/autodoc/page/kin1int-1
(Academy of Achievement, "Coretta Scott King," undated)

http://www.thekingcenter.org/csk/bio.html
(TheKingCenter.com, "Mrs. Coretta Scott King, Human Rights Activist and Leader," undated)
http://www.time.com/time/archive/printout/0,23657,901556,00.html
(Time.com, "Bearing Witness," Oct. 3, 1969, archived article)

Online Databases

Biography Resource Center Online, 2006, articles from *Contemporary Authors Online*, 2006, *Contemporary Black Biography*, 1992, and *Notable Black American Women*, 1992

WORLD WIDE WEB SITE

http://www.thekingcenter.org

Cesar Millan 1969?-

Mexican Dog Behavior Specialist
Star of the TV Series "The Dog Whisperer"

BIRTH

Cesar Millan was born around 1969 in Culiacan, Mexico, during a hurricane that tore the roof off his family's house. His mother, Maria Teresa Favela d'Millan, was a seamstress. His father, Felipe Millan Guillen, was a newspaper deliveryman and photographer. Millan has one brother and several sisters. He was especially close to his grandfather, Teodoro Millan Angulo, as he was growing up.

YOUTH

Millan and his family lived in Culiacan much of the time. But he spent his childhood weekends and summers on his grandparents' farm in Ixpalino, Mexico, about an hour from his house. The farm had no electricity, and he woke up before the sun rose. Mexico had many farms or ranches that were owned by the patrones, who were wealthy, while the land was worked by the campesinos, who rented the land and earned little. Millan's grandfather was a campesino. He took care of cattle for the patrones, and the family also raised chickens and other animals for their own sustenance.

"The only place I really wanted to be was among the animals. From as early as I can remember, I loved to spend hours walking with them or just silently watching them, trying to figure out how their wild minds worked. . . . I never thought of them as the same as us, but I can't remember ever thinking animals were 'less' than us, either. I was always endlessly fascinated —and delighted—by our differences."

When Millan was growing up, most people he knew were working class and did not have much money, so he never felt poor. His grandparents' four-room house on the farm was crowded with his siblings and cousins, but Millan thought the place was paradise and that he belonged there, close to the animals. He recalled his early connection to them in his book *Cesar's Way*: "The only place I really wanted to be was among the animals. From as early as I can remember, I loved to spend hours walking with them or just silently watching them, trying to figure out how their wild minds worked. Whether it was a cat, a chicken, a bull, or a goat, I wanted to know what the world looked like through the eyes of each animal—and I wanted to understand that animal from the inside out. I never thought of them as the same as us, but I can't remember ever thinking animals were 'less' than us, either. I was always endlessly fascinated—and delighted—by our differences."

On the farm, Millan learned that in order for the dogs to live in harmony with the family—working willingly and remaining calm and submissive —the humans had to establish their role as pack leaders. His grandfather's dogs always walked beside or behind him, and his grandfather never resorted to violence, bribery, or raising his voice. His confidence and even temperament projected dominance over the pack and Millan observed this and learned to imitate him.

Millan had plenty of opportunity to spend time with dogs. He was always comfortable around them, and he found that the dogs were content when the humans exuded this confidence. He explained how this early exposure to dogs shaped his future with them: "In our family, having dogs around was like having water to drink. Canines were a constant presence in my childhood, and I can't overstate their importance to my development in becoming the man I am today. I wouldn't want to imagine a world that didn't have dogs in it. I respect dogs' dignity as proud and miraculous animals. . . . To say that I 'love' dogs doesn't even come close to describing my deep feelings and affinity for them."

Moving to the Big City

Educational opportunities were lacking in Culiacan, where the family lived. So when Cesar was about six years old, the family moved to the large coastal city of Mazatlan, where Millan's father took a job delivering newspapers. At first, the family lived in a small apartment. This new living arrangement was not suitable for dogs, as the animals were accustomed to running free and the city was crowded and the streets were busy. Most of the dogs in the resort town where the family now lived were scavengers, and people mistreated them. Millan didn't like city life, where his mom worried about him walking just to the corner and he was separated from nature and the animals on the farm. The weekends spent on the farm could not come quickly enough for him.

Once he was hired as a photographer for the government, Millan's father bought the family a nice home near the ocean. But Cesar still longed to find his place in the big city. He started following a local doctor who regularly walked his purebred Irish setter. It was the first purebred dog Millan had ever seen, and he was mesmerized. When the dog had puppies, Millan asked the doctor for one of the dogs, and the man refused. Purebred puppies were valuable, and Millan was just a kid. Two years later, the doctor granted his wish and gave him a puppy from one of the Irish setter's litters. Saluki became his constant companion.

Fitting In

While Millan made fast friends with his canine companion, he felt out of place around his peers in Mazatlan. But he tried to fit in. Using his dog pack mentality, Millan made attempts to submit to the "pack" of city kids

who were not so accepting of the boy from the country. "I hung out with them and went with them to the beach, played baseball and soccer, but deep inside I knew I was faking it. It was never like on the farm, chasing a frog here and there, catching fireflies in jars and then setting them free, or simply sitting under the stars, listening to the crickets' song. Nature had always offered me something new to learn, something to think about. Sports were just working off energy and trying to fit in."

It wasn't until his parents enrolled him in judo classes that he felt he had something special to connect to away from the farm. By the time he was 14, Millan had won six judo championships in a row, and he learned many techniques that would later serve him as a dog psychologist—single-mindedness, self-control, quieting the mind, and deep concentration. He credits his parents with finding the perfect outlet for his frustration with living in a place where he felt like a stranger. "Only when I was with Mother Nature or doing judo was I truly in my element."

EDUCATION

Growing up in Mexico, Millan attended local schools in Culiacan and Mazatlan. Despite his proficiency with dogs, he has had little formal education and is entirely self-taught.

FIRST JOBS

When Millan was a teenager, his classmates began discussing what careers they would like to have when they grew up. Millan knew he wanted a job that had something to do with dogs. He had been enthralled by the television shows "Lassie" and "Rin Tin Tin," which were filmed in English and dubbed in Spanish. He learned that dog trainers were standing offscreen, directing the dogs' actions, and he thought he had found his calling. His dream of becoming the best dog trainer in the world was born. "Saying to myself 'I'm gong to work with dogs and be the best trainer in the world' felt to me like being given a glass of water after nearly dying of thirst. If felt *natural*, easy, and it felt really *good*. Suddenly, I wasn't fighting myself anymore. I knew the path I would take on the way to my future."

To begin working toward his new career goal, Millan got a job at a local veterinarian's office at the age of 15. He started with sweeping and cleaning up after the animals, quickly moved to grooming, and then became a veterinary technician. His employers realized his gift with dogs, and he was enlisted to control dogs even the veterinarian didn't want to approach.

During Millan's time at the vet's office he was dubbed "El Perrero," or "The Dog Boy," by his peers. This was not a complimentary nickname, as Mexican dogs in the big cities were considered filthy and a nuisance. Millan was treated the same as the dogs he loved. "Did I care? No. I was on a mission."

"Saying to myself 'I'm gong to work with dogs and be the best trainer in the world' felt to me like being given a glass of water after nearly dying of thirst. If felt natural, *easy, and it felt really* good. *Suddenly, I wasn't fighting myself anymore. I knew the path I would take on the way to my future."*

CAREER HIGHLIGHTS

Crossing the Border

The next step in Millan's mission was immigrating to the United States when he was about 21. To legally emigrate from Mexico, a large sum of money is needed for a visa. Raising that much money is nearly impossible for working-class Mexicans. So over a half-million Mexicans instead enter the United States illegally every year. The U.S. government has made great efforts to curb this trend, citing overcrowding and the loss of jobs for American citizens.

After three failed attempts to cross the border on his own, Millan decided to use a coyote—someone who helps Mexicans illegally cross the border into the United States. He paid the coyote the entire $100 he had with him to get him out of Mexico. The trip was harrowing. They ran to the point of exhaustion, froze in a water hole for hours, and mucked through mud. Once across the border, the coyote gave a taxi driver in the States $20 of Millan's money, and sent him on his way. "Fortunately, the taxi driver spoke Spanish, because I knew not one word of English. He drove me to San Diego and dropped me off there—dripping wet, filthy, thirsty, hungry, my boots covered with mud. I was the happiest man in the world. I was in the U.S." Millan later paid a fee to the U.S. government for his illegal crossing, and he is now a U.S. citizen.

"

"Unconsciously, I was beginning to apply the dog psychology I had learned on my grandfather's farm. I was interacting with the dogs the way they interacted with one another. This was the birth of the rehabilitation methods I still use today, although I couldn't have explained in words what I was doing at the time—neither in English nor in Spanish. Everything I did just came instinctually to me."

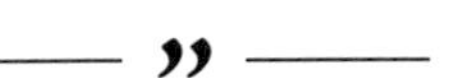

Working with Dogs

Millan's first words of English were "Do you have a job application?" He had lived on the streets for over a month when he was hired by the owners of a dog grooming parlor. He has called these two women his American guardian angels, as they hired him despite his filthy appearance and his inability to speak English. Once they learned he was homeless, the angels allowed him to live in the store. "Believe me, not a day goes by that I don't remember how truly blessed I've been with the people who've been put in my path."

His next stop was Los Angeles, where Millan began working at a dog training establishment. Clients brought their dogs here to learn commands such as sit, stay, and heel. Millan did not agree with the center's methods of training, and he began to feel the urge to implement his own ideas. He felt that intimidation and fear were not effective means to train dogs and that an understanding of the animals' psychology would provide much better results.

Instead of yelling at the troubled dogs, Millan was quiet and did not touch or look directly at them when he first approached. His position as leader was established this way, as in a natural setting, where the dog that is calm and assertive becomes the leader and is followed by the other animals. "Unconsciously, I was beginning to apply the dog psychology I had

Millan enjoying time outside with his dogs.

learned on my grandfather's farm. I was interacting with the dogs the way they interacted with one another. This was the birth of the rehabilitation methods I still use today, although I couldn't have explained in words what I was doing at the time—neither in English nor in Spanish. Everything I did just came instinctually to me."

Lessons in Business

While Millan was working at the center, one of his clients hired him away to wash his fleet of limousines. This change of direction for Millan proved invaluable, as he learned the ins and outs of running a business from his new boss. Part of his compensation was the use of a minivan, and he considered this a very big deal. "I didn't have the pink slip—but for me, it symbolized the first time I truly felt I had 'made it' in America."

Once Millan had use of a vehicle, he started his own dog training business, called Pacific Point Canine Academy. His new goal was not to train movie dogs in Hollywood but to help regular dogs and their owners build better relationships. His new boss knew many people and helped spread the word about Millan's training abilities. "He'd call up his friends and say, 'I've got this great Mexican guy who's amazing with dogs. Just bring 'em over.'"

Working with the owner is an important part of dog training.

The business took off, and in 1998 Millan purchased two acres of property in a tough neighborhood of South Los Angeles to establish his business, the Dog Psychology Center. At the Center, he worked with his clients' dogs and took in orphaned dogs that were likely to be euthanized. One of his early customers was actress Jada Pinkett Smith, who became a mentor to Millan. She referred him to her friends and hired an English tutor for him. "I knew that the minute he was able to articulate what he does, he was going to fly," Pinkett Smith said. "I've always known there was no way in the world he wasn't going to accomplish what he wanted to. Cesar is a go-getter and a hard worker."

Through his broken but improving English, Millan set out to teach people how to behave with their dogs. He wanted to help people understand that they should not treat dogs like humans. "Thinking back to my natural relationship with them [dogs], I began to see how I could help dogs in the United States become happier, healthier creatures—and help their owners, too.... My fulfillment formula is simple: for a balanced, healthy dog, a human must share exercise, discipline, and affection, in that order!" It was then that Cesar began his daily ritual of walking the dogs from the center, off leash, on hours-long treks through the neighborhood. People commented, "It's like watching the Pied Piper go by."

A Television Series

After being featured in the *Los Angeles Times,* Millan was pursued by Hollywood producers who wanted to showcase his talents on television. He eventually sold his series, "The Dog Whisperer," to the National Geographic Channel. The weekly half-hour program debuted in 2004 and was hugely successful. In 2006, the series was expanded to hour-long episodes.

On "The Dog Whisperer," Millan rehabilitates dogs and trains people. He shows people who have had trouble with their dogs how to become the pack leader, through calm, assertive energy. He stresses with every client the need to walk their dog, provide rules and boundaries, and give rewards only when the dog is in a submissive state. The *Los Angeles Times* said the following in a review of his show: "His brand of tough love is simple. He avoids condescension or blame while gently, unequivocally informing people that they've been selfish and insensitive to their dog's needs. . . . Whether he's in front of a camera or not, Millan has the bearing of a leader. His gaze is direct, his posture commanding. He's a superb mimic and can snarl, scratch, pant and yip with the best (or worst) of them as he assumes the demeanor of an excited or fearful dog."

"

"His brand of tough love is simple. He avoids condescension or blame while gently, unequivocally informing people that they've been selfish and insensitive to their dog's needs.... Whether he's in front of a camera or not, Millan has the bearing of a leader. His gaze is direct, his posture commanding. He's a superb mimic and can snarl, scratch, pant, and yip with the best (or worst) of them as he assumes the demeanor of an excited or fearful dog."

—the Los Angeles Times

"

On the show, Millan has gone to the homes of the owners without prior information and has supervised remarkable transformations in both humans and dogs. He helped Buddy the beagle's owners help him overcome his fear of the garden hose and showed bulldog Matilda's family how to keep her from chasing skateboards. He spent two days at a women's correctional facility where the inmates foster troubled dogs, and he taught actress Daisy Fuentes how to become the pack leader for her English bulldog, Alfie.

Millan has taken his training message to dog owners across the country through several different means. In addition to his work on television, he has also conducted live seminars for dogs and their owners. He wrote a book, *Cesar's Way: The Natural, Everyday Guide to Understanding and Correcting Common Dog Problems,* which was published in 2006. He has also been the author of a bi-weekly column for the web site www.pets911.com. He has called Oprah Winfrey "the number one role model for my own professional behavior" and has appeared several times on her television program, "The Oprah Winfrey Show." He has said of Winfrey, "In the human world, she is not only always in charge, she is also amazingly calm and even-tempered."

MARRIAGE AND FAMILY

Ilusion Wilson Millan was just 16 when she and Cesar began dating. He was over 21. He was told by a friend that U.S. law made it illegal for him to have a girlfriend who was so young. Afraid of being arrested and deported, Millan broke off their relationship. Ilusion sought him out when she turned 18, and they were married. Millan says he learned a lot from his wife about how to be a better husband. Having grown up in a patriarchal household, Millan acted dominant and jealous, behavior that reflected what he experienced in Mexico. That behavior created problems in his marriage: Ilusion left him and would only reconcile when he agreed to marriage counseling. "You know," he admitted, "it took a long time for me to actually let go of this machismo thing. Machismo allows you to be ignorant, stupid, dumb. You know, all the bad things. So you're not really sensitive to the person. It's all about you."

The Millans have two sons, Andre and Calvin. He does feel it is proper, in fact necessary, to show dominance in his role as a father. "Watch 'Nanny 911' or any of those shows—kids who get nothing but affection are impossible to deal with. . . . What they really need to do is run around the block and then do their homework. Just like dogs, if you don't take a dominant position over your kids, they'll take a dominant position over you."

SELECTED WRITINGS

Cesar's Way: The Natural, Everyday Guide to Understanding and Correcting Common Dog Problems, 2006 (with Melissa Jo Peltier)

SELECTED CREDITS

Videos

People Training for Dogs, 2005
Becoming a Pack Leader, 2006

Television

"The Dog Whisperer," 2004-

FURTHER READING

Periodicals

El Andar Magazine, Summer 2001, p.42
Latina, Sep. 2005, p.100
Los Angeles Times, Oct. 18, 2004, p.E1
Men's Health, May 2005, p.104
People, Dec.9, 2002, p.199
San Diego Union-Tribune, Oct. 17, 2004, p.F1

ADDRESS

Cesar Millan
Dog Psychology Center of Los Angeles
919 East 61st Street
Los Angeles, CA 90001

WORLD WIDE WEB SITES

http://www.dogpsychologycenter.com
http://www.nationalgeographic.com/channel/dogwhisperer

Nick Park 1958-

British Writer, Director, and Producer of Animated Films
Oscar-Winning Creator of the Wallace and Gromit Movies and *Chicken Run*

BIRTH

Nicholas Wulstan Park, known as Nick Park, was born on December 6, 1958, in Preston, the capital of county Lancashire in northwest England. He was the middle child of Roger Park, a professional photographer, and Celia Park, a dressmaker. Nick grew up with three brothers, Adrian, Andrew, and Adam, and one sister, Janet.

YOUTH

Park was interested in art from a very young age. His parents and teachers encouraged him to develop his talent, so young Nick had hours of free time to just draw, doodle, and create. Being known as the class artist "was a good boost because I was absolutely rubbish at everything else," he recalled. "I didn't do well academically. I'm a very slow reader. But I liked writing stories." He found many ways to exercise his imagination. He collected old toys and machine parts and kept them in a box under his bed. "I used to call it 'my box of useful things' and I used to talk with my brothers about how one day we'd be able to build a rocket or a time machine if we kept all these bits and pieces."

Park's family also provided him with inspiration. His father was a commercial photographer who spent hours at home building things. His mother was also creative, sewing clothes for the family. Once the elder Parks created a camping trailer from a box and a set of wheels. The trailer came complete with furniture and wallpaper on the interior to make it feel cozy, and the family used it on a trip to Wales. This "do-it-yourself" inventiveness would inspire young Nick's first attempts at animation, as well as his most famous characters, Wallace and Gromit.

> *Park collected old toys and machine parts and kept them in a box under his bed. "I used to call it 'my box of useful things' and I used to talk with my brothers about how one day we'd be able to build a rocket or a time machine if we kept all these bits and pieces."*

As a youth, Park was fascinated with animated films and began experimenting with the format. His first attempt was a zoetrope, which creates the illusion of animation by spinning images on a cylinder. He submitted the zoetrope to a cereal-box contest in hopes of winning a movie camera, but failed to win anything. The disappointment didn't stop him, especially after he discovered his mother's standard 8mm movie camera had a "single frame" button. By using this button to shoot one frame of film at a time, Park created his first animated work. "Walter the Rat" was shot from a book of drawings, but the film was ruined during processing. Despite this disappointment, the aspiring animator continued making short films during his spare time. He experimented with paper cutouts, puppets, clay figures, and homemade cels (transparent pages) in his films, which he shared with family and friends.

By the time Park was in his teens, he was gaining attention for his hobby. His teachers encouraged him to screen his work at school. "When the school found out I did [films], they insisted I show them at assembly," the animator recalled. "People loved it, which was great because I loved making people laugh, but wasn't much by way of a performer." At age 15, he entered a short film, "Archie's Concrete Nightmare," in a competition for young animators sponsored by the British Broadcasting Corporation (BBC). Although he failed to win a prize, the BBC still aired the film on nationwide television. According to Park, "I received instant fame in my school at the age of 15; I thought I had reached the pinnacle of my career."

Park was quite young when one of his short films was broadcast on national television. "I received instant fame in my school at the age of 15; I thought I had reached the pinnacle of my career."

EDUCATION

After finishing secondary school, Park took a series of arts courses, fearing it would be too difficult to break into the film industry. He learned art techniques from sculpture to stained glass and then entered Sheffield Polytechnic (now part of Sheffield Hallam University), one of Britain's top art schools. When his advisors learned of his filmmaking hobby, they encouraged him to take classes that would support it. He majored in communication arts and completed his Bachelor of Arts (BA) degree in 1980. During his time at Sheffield he completed an animated film of "Jack and the Beanstalk," using chalk images drawn on a blackboard. The film earned him a prize in a student competition and also won him a spot in Britain's National Film and Television School (NFTS).

At the NFTS, Park spent his first year learning the basics of filmmaking: lighting, camera work, sound, and editing. After completing these classes he specialized in animation and began working on a 35mm film to help fulfill his graduation requirements. He wrote a script about an inventor who builds a rocket and travels to the moon with the help of his dog. He decided to work in Plasticine, a synthetic modeling clay that stays pliable in air but won't melt under film lights. He also decided to use stop-motion technique, a very labor-intensive and time-consuming way to make a movie.

In stop-motion technique, the filmmaker sets up a scene using models and then uses a special camera to take a picture of the scene. Then the filmmaker makes a tiny adjustment to the figures and takes another picture. The filmmaker continues this way—move the object, take a picture, move the object, take a picture. Each of those pictures becomes a single frame of film, and just one second of movie film requires 24 frames. When the frames are linked together and shown continuously, the object appear to move. To show a character walking through a door, for example, might require a hundred or more frames of film. For each of those frames, Park would have to adjust the positions of the door, the character's arms and legs, and the character's facial features, in order to create the illusion of movement and expression.

Unfortunately, when Park decided to use stop-motion technique, the NFTS didn't have a camera suitable for model animation; it wasn't until his third year there that they could supply him with the right equipment. It took him another year to film the first page of his script, as he had to change each model's position for every single frame of film. He graduated from the NFTS in 1983 but stayed to work on the film. He was running low on time and money when the NFTS helped him meet some film industry contacts that offered him a way to finish it. Animators Peter Lord and David Sproxton came to speak at the NFTS, and they became interested in Park's work. They not only offered him a job, but the chance to finish his film.

CAREER HIGHLIGHTS

An Award-Winning Debut

In 1985, Park began working at Aardman Animation, which Lord and Sproxton had founded in 1976. He moved to Bristol, England, and used Aardman's facilities to continue filming his story of a trip to the moon. Splitting his time between his duties for Aardman and his own project, it took Park another four years to complete a film just over 20 minutes long. (At 24 frames of film per second, that meant posing and shooting around 30,000 separate scenes of his Plasticine models.) *A Grand Day Out* finally debuted in 1989 and introduced Park's signature characters, Wallace the inventor and his dog, Gromit. In *A Grand Day Out,* Wallace decides he would like to vacation on the moon, since it is made of his very favorite thing: cheese. He builds a spaceship—Gromit contributing to the construction by hammering, drilling, welding, and painting—and the two travel into space. During their visit to the moon, they nibble on the cheesy landscape (with crackers, of course) and meet a lonely robot before returning home.

Wallace and Gromit made their first appearance in the 1989 short film A Grand Day Out.

A Grand Day Out introduced Wallace and Gromit and also established Park's signature style: intricate gadgets to provide action; amusing visual details; and incredibly expressive characters who can communicate a wealth of emotion by just moving an eyebrow. Gromit never speaks or smiles (his model doesn't even have a mouth), but viewers can easily understand his exasperation when Wallace uses him as a sawhorse or drips paint on his head. The lunar robot, which looks like a strange, coin-operated oven, uses only a pair of metal arms to express emotions from puzzlement and surprise to panic and despair. These complete characters give depth to the story, while clever visuals—Wallace's first scribbles at his drawing board are really games of tic-tac-toe; the inside of the spaceship looks like the inside of the house—create laugh-out-loud moments of enjoyment. *A Grand Day Out* won several animation awards, including best short animated film from the British Academy for Film and Television Arts (BAFTA) in 1990 and an Academy Award ("Oscar") nomination for best animated short film from the Academy of Motion Picture Arts and Sciences in 1991.

Although *A Grand Day Out* lost at the 1991 Academy Awards, Park could not be disappointed: the winner that year was another of his creations, the five-minute short *Creature Comforts.* This Plasticine stop-motion film was completed as part of his work for Aardman. In his work there he had performed animation for commercials and television shows such as *The Amazing Adventures of Morph;* he also contributed to Aardman's groundbreaking music video for Peter Gabriel's number-one hit "Sledgehammer."

Creature Comforts was part of a series of short animated films Aardman produced for British television's Channel 4. First aired in 1989, the film presents several zoo animals being interviewed about their living conditions. While the voices sound like everyday people, the visuals are full of Park's usual inventive detail. A jungle cat complains of the cold and damp; the youngest member of a polar bear family enjoys their habitat; a chicken speaks of the superiority of zoo life to the circus life of her sisters; an ape relates the boredom of captivity; and a turtle finds excitement in reading. "I found that almost anybody's conversation is funny if you put it in an animal's mouth, because you can have the animals doing things that the humans were not," Park explained. "You can have fun changing the context." Besides winning an Oscar, *Creature Comforts* earned a BAFTA Award nomination in 1990 (losing to *A Grand Day Out*) and several animation festival prizes. In 2003, Aardman expanded the original *Creature Comforts* into a multi-part series for British television.

"I found that almost anybody's conversation is funny if you put it in an animal's mouth, because you can have the animals doing things that the humans were not," Park explained. "You can have fun changing the context."

Wallace & Gromit Captivate Audiences

After the success of his first films, Park had the freedom to continue creating his own animated stories. He decided that Wallace and Gromit would star in another adventure, titled *The Wrong Trousers,* but this time he wanted to improve on both the plot and the animation. "I've always thought of myself as a filmmaker first and foremost," Park commented. "With *The Wrong Trousers,* I wanted to do something much more complex and ambitious." He decided to design, light, and film the models as if they were live-action film sets. "I really wanted *The Wrong Trousers* to have the look of a mini-feature film with Hitchcockian and B-movie references thrown in." Aardman and the BBC invested almost £700,000 (over $1 million) in the 13-month shoot.

When it debuted on TV during the 1993 Christmas season, the 30-minute film captivated critics and audiences. *The Wrong Trousers* opens on Gromit's birthday, with the dog hoping for a nice present from Wallace (voiced by British actor Peter Sallis). Instead, he gets a pair of "techno-trousers" that can take him for walks. The gift leaves Wallace's piggy bank empty, so he

Park on the set of The Wrong Trousers, *with Feathers McGraw in the background, 1994.*

decides to rent out a room in their house. Unfortunately, their new boarder is the notorious criminal Feathers McGraw, a penguin who has evil plans for Wallace and the techno-trousers. Although Gromit is driven away from the house by the penguin, he comes to Wallace's rescue, saving the day after an amazing model train chase.

The Wrong Trousers demonstrated the technical improvements Park had made in design, animation, light, and sound. But it was the film's story, wit, and visual details that made it a hit. There are sly references to the pair's previous adventure: Gromit's newspaper proclaims "Moon cheese shares soar!"; replicas of their spaceship decorate the living room wall; and Feathers McGraw uses Gromit's copy of *Electronics for Dogs* to take control of the techno-trousers. There are fantastic inventions, including the device to get Wallace dressed in the morning that ends up trapping him in the techno-trousers. And there are witty visual jokes, such as the books titled *Sheep* and *Sticks* in Gromit's doghouse, or the billboard for sleeping pills that Wallace passes as he sleepwalks in the techno-trousers. The fun is underpinned by Wallace and Gromit's relationship: viewers can feel Gromit's sadness when the penguin takes his place in the home, as well as Wallace's relief when Gromit comes to rescue him. *The Wrong Trousers* was the top-rated TV program in Britain during the 1993 holiday season, and it also won audience and jury prizes at festivals around the world. In 1994 it won both the BAFTA Award and the Academy Award for best short animated film.

Audiences wanted more Wallace and Gromit, so the BBC commissioned a third adventure for broadcast on Christmas Day 1995. Park had only 18 months to write, design, and animate the duo's next adventure, so he ended up turning over much of the animation to staff at Aardman. He taught them the "style" of animating Wallace and Gromit, and found other time-saving measures. For instance, the filmmaker noted, "we pre-make all the mouth shapes, 'a', 'e', 'i', 'o', 'u' and all the other consonants, and we can replace the mouths each time and smooth it over. But even with that we have to watch that it doesn't look too mechanical." Being more of a supervisor was a challenge for Park, he revealed: "I found it quite frustrating not doing much animation myself and it was odd seeing other people handling my ideas." Nevertheless, when *A Close Shave* aired in 1995, it was unmistakably Park's creation. In this 30-minute adventure, a stray sheep leads Wallace and Gromit to discover who has been rustling local flocks and causing a yarn shortage. When Gromit is framed for the crime, it's up to Wallace to rescue his dog—as well as local yarn shop owner Wendolene Ramsbottom, who may be involved in the plot.

Like previous Wallace and Gromit films, *A Close Shave* is packed with interesting inventions, including Wallace's window-cleaning gadgets and the combination sheep-shearing/ sweater-making "Knit-O-Matic" machine stolen by the villain. It has amazing action sequences, including a car chase with a dozen sheep riding Wallace's motorcycle. And it has plenty of visual jokes for the observant viewer, such as the evil dog Preston's *Telegruff* newspaper (a take-off on the name of the famous British paper the *Telegraph*), or the copy of *Crime and Punishment* by "Fido Dogstoyevsky" (a take-off on the name of the Russian author Fyodor Dostoyevsky) that Gromit reads while in jail. This attention to detail is deliberate, the filmmaker observed: "I'm glad [when people] notice those little things, that's what I hope for. I want the films to have a personal touch to them, a kind of handmade quality." *A Close Shave* earned Park his third trophies for best animated film at both the BAFTA Awards and the Academy Awards, plus another nine awards at film festivals around the world.

Although short films rarely get seen outside of occasional television and festival appearances, Park's Wallace and Gromit films were finding many fans. Videos of the pair's adventures were translated into 20 languages and sold well throughout the world, especially in the United States and Japan. Merchandising of Wallace and Gromit took off, with products from clocks and clothing to stuffed animals available to fans. Wallace's mention of Wensleydale cheese even saved one dairy that produced it from bankruptcy. Although he wants to keep the characters associated with quality items, Park noted the merchandising is "quite thrilling, be-

Wallace and Gromit in a scene from A Close Shave. *Park accidentally left the models of Wallace and Gromit in the trunk of a New York City cab during a press trip, but they were recovered after frantic appeals in the press.*

cause I always dreamt I would create something that would be popular." When Park accidentally left models of Wallace and Gromit in a New York taxi during a press tour, it made headlines in Britain and America. Luckily, two days later the cab driver located and returned the Plasticine figures, worth $10,000.

Making a Feature-Length Film

Park and his colleagues at Aardman were interested in branching out into feature films, and with Wallace and Gromit's Oscar wins they were able to secure the financial backing. They entered a deal with the American studio DreamWorks (which produced the popular *Shrek* animated films) to co-produce Aardman's first full-length movie. Park did not want to rush Wallace and Gromit into a feature film without a solid story behind them; instead he pitched the idea of an escape movie starring chickens. His partners loved the concept, and Park and co-director Peter Lord began the long process of directing *Chicken Run.* With over 115,000 frames of film to shoot, they "split direction down the middle, because we worked on the original idea together and the storyboards [so] each knew what the other wanted," Park explained.

> *"I'm glad [when people] notice those little things, that's what I hope for. I want the films to have a personal touch to them, a kind of handmade quality."*

In the film, a group of chickens are living at the Tweedy farm. Ginger (voiced by Julia Sawalha) tries to lead her fellow chickens to freedom from Mrs. Tweedy's dreaded pie machine. Her attempts are thwarted until the appearance of Rocky (voiced by Mel Gibson), an American stunt rooster she believes can teach them to fly. Much of the story of *Chicken Run* drew on Park's own teenaged experiences working in a chicken-packing factory. One day he staffed the slaughterhouse, where "chickens were hung up by their feet and they'd peck at the shackles." For a young man who grew up with pet chickens in his house, "it was absolutely horrible," Park remembered, and thus certain scenes in the film resemble classic horror films. *Chicken Run* also recalls such famous World War II prison movies as the 1963 classic *The Great Escape;* other sequences mirror such adventure films as *Raiders of the Lost Ark.*

When *Chicken Run* debuted in 2000, it charmed both audiences and critics. The Plasticine stop-motion animation and the lack of child characters or musical numbers made it different from most animated films. With its superb comic timing and eye-popping action, it was a family film that all ages could enjoy. As a result, *Chicken Run* received many awards for best animated film of the year, including awards from the National Board of Review, the Broadcast Film Critics Association, and the International Press Academy. It was also nominated for the Golden Globe for best mu-

In this scene from Chicken Run, *Ginger and Rocky are trapped in Mrs. Tweedy's dreaded pie machine.*

sical/comedy and the BAFTA Award for best British film, in both cases competing against live-action films. (The film received no Academy Award nominations, as there was no best animated feature Oscar until the following year.) *Chicken Run* was also a financial success, earning over $100 million at the U.S. box office and almost $225 million worldwide. DreamWorks was so pleased with the film that shortly before its debut they announced they would collaborate with Aardman on another four feature films.

Wallace and Gromit Return

Much to the delight of fans, when Aardman and DreamWorks announced their next project, it was to be a full-length Wallace and Gromit film. "[A full-length] film always seemed like a natural step," Park explained. "But part of the reason why we did *Chicken Run* first is because I was naturally a bit cautious. What happens in a short-film format often works because it is short. We were really waiting for the right idea to come along." Creating a feature film meant Park and co-director Steve Box had to turn over animation of the pair to the staff at Aardman. To get them familiar with the characters, "every week we have Wallace and Gromit classes where everybody has to do exercises with Wallace and Gromit, just to get into character." The animators also trained by creating a series of ten two-minute films about Wallace's wild inventions, called "Cracking Contraptions." These debuted on the BBC during Christmas 2002, and the following year *Wallace & Gromit: The Curse of the Were-Rabbit* began filming. Even with between 20 and 30 animators working on over 30 different sets, the film took three years to finish.

The Curse of the Were-Rabbit, which debuted in 2005, is a tribute to such classic horror movies as *Frankenstein, Dracula,* and *The Wolf Man.* Park called it the "world's first vegetarian horror film" because the only things in jeopardy are the town's prize vegetables. Wallace and Gromit's humane pest control business, "Anti-Pesto," is getting plenty of action as their town gets ready for the annual vegetable competition at Lady Tottington's estate. When the bunnies they trap start filling up their basement, Wallace attempts to brainwash them out of their love for vegetables. His "Mind Manipulation-O-Matic" goes wrong, however, and creates a giant rabbit that terrorizes the town. Lady Tottington's suitor, the sinister Victor, believes a gun is the best way to handle the situation, leaving it up to Gromit to save the day in another fantastic chase sequence. The film also continues the tradition of visual jokes: when Wallace becomes stuck in his dressing machine, a jar of "Middle Age Spread" is seen at the breakfast table; a bookcase with volumes titled *Swiss Cheese Family Robinson* and *Grated Expectations* hides his stash of cheese.

"There is no worse situation to be in than Oscar night," Park noted. "It's not the winning or losing, just the fact that you might have to get up and say something in front of every famous face you've ever seen."

The film was a critical and financial success, opening in October 2005 at No. 1 in the U.S. box office. Unfortunately, that same weekend an electrical fire at an Aardman warehouse destroyed most of the original drawings, storyboards, and sets Park used in the first Wallace and Gromit films and in *Chicken Run.* Park considered himself lucky because no one was injured and current studio projects were unaffected. Still, the news coverage of the event moved him: "It sort of said, 'This is an important part of British film history.' I never knew that was how it was being valued, so that was quite nice." He was also pleasantly surprised when *Curse of the Were-Rabbit* was nominated for the best British film at the 2006 BAFTA Awards, especially after it beat out such "proper films" as *The Constant Gardener* and *Pride and Prejudice* to win the trophy. When the Academy Awards were presented the next month, it was no surprise that Wallace and Gromit walked away with the Oscar for best animated feature film, bringing Park's total to four. Despite his success in Hollywood, "there is no worse situation to be in than Oscar night. Not knowing whether you've won is completely draining," Park noted. "It's not the winning or losing, just the fact that you might have to get up and say something in front of every famous face you've ever seen."

"

"I see myself in both of them actually," Park said about his famous characters. "They're both opposites. There's a kind of tension, you know, Gromit wanting the quiet life and order and Wallace constantly going off on tangents and causing chaos and getting mad ideas."

"

The worldwide success of his films sometimes amazes Park, because Wallace and Gromit seem so particularly British in their humor and setting. In creating the films, he said, "we just did what made us laugh, instinctively, and we never really thought about age groups and targeting certain people." But viewers all over the world can understand the realistic relationship—almost like that of a long-married couple—that underlies Wallace and Gromit's adventures. "I see myself in both of them actually," the filmmaker admitted. "They're both opposites. There's a kind of tension, you know, Gromit wanting the quiet life and order and Wallace constantly going off on tangents and causing chaos and getting mad ideas." In playing off this emotional tension, Park can make films that are "about the real world," the filmmaker remarked. "Things are cruel, life is cruel: people are inconsistent and they do things without realizing." Gromit is "more human than Wallace. . . . He's more aware and more emotional. He carries with him all these doubts about Wallace—you know he's been hurt in the past." It is this emphasis on character that ultimately explains Wallace and Gromit's worldwide appeal.

Park has begun experimenting with computer-generated graphics, or CG animation, working on a film tentatively called *Flushed Away* about a penthouse rat whisked down to a sewer. But Plasticine still remains his medi-

Wallace and Gromit and the Anti-Pesto SWAT Team are on the case, in a scene from Wallace & Gromit: The Curse of the Were-Rabbit.

um of choice. The chunky arms and lopsided smiles it creates are suited to his sense of humor. "I love working with models," he said. "Basically what you've got is a puppet in front of a camera. There's a certain amount of improvisation. Other techniques, like drawn animation, especially with computers, you've got the chance to keep perfecting it. Here, you've got to play it by ear a lot—go for it." It may sometimes look old-fashioned, but Park explained that "we don't mind fingerprints on the characters—they're real, made from real materials." The future will most likely include more adventures for Wallace and Gromit, the director has stated, but his first concern is to find a great story to tell. "My animation has developed over the years but my fascination for the magic of animation which began at 13 has remained unchanged."

HOME AND FAMILY

Never married, Park lives alone in a 150-year-old cottage not far from the Aardman studios in Bristol, England. Interestingly, the filmmaker has never owned a dog, not even as a child. "I never had a dog," he explained. Better behaved—and quieter—than any real-life pet, "[Gromit is] the dog I never had."

MAJOR INFLUENCES

Park cites many moviemakers as inspiration for his work, including suspense film director Alfred Hitchcock and animators Walt Disney, Tex Avery (creator of Daffy Duck and Bugs Bunny's phrase "What's Up, Doc?"), and Chuck Jones (creator of the Road Runner and Wile E. Coyote). The works of American Ray Harryhausen, however, really stand out. Harryhausen's films used stop-motion animation to depict famous myths and legends, creating such monsters as fighting skeletons, a dragon, a one-eyed Cyclops, and a Hydra, a serpent with many heads. "I have memories of one Christmas Eve, cosily watching the TV, 10 years old, and [seeing Harryhausen's 1951 short] *Hansel and Gretel*," Park recalled. "I just loved it completely for its quality and at the time I was starting to dabble in animation. . . . I didn't really know how it was done, but I just loved the feeling of it, and it just remained with me."

Park has never owned a dog, not even as a child. "I never had a dog," he explained. "[Gromit is] the dog I never had."

HOBBIES AND OTHER INTERESTS

Park's work-intensive films leave him little free time, but he does enjoy walks in the British countryside. He also lends his time and characters to charities. In 1995, Wallace and Gromit's "Grand Appeal" was established to raise funds for a new children's hospital in Bristol. In 1997, the charity sponsored the first "Wrong Trousers Day," asking ordinary citizens to contribute to their fund and wear crazy-looking pants; that year they raised £500,000 (over $900,000). From 2000 to 2002, similar events raised money for seven other children's hospitals and hospices in Britain. In 2003, the Wallace and Gromit's Children's Foundation was established, making "Wrong Trousers Day" an annual event across Britain. Park serves as a patron of this charity (online at http://www.wallaceandgromitfoundation.org).

MOVIES

Short Films; Writer and Director

A Grand Day Out, 1989
Creature Comforts, 1989
The Wrong Trousers, 1993 (written with Bob Baker)
A Close Shave, 1995 (written with Bob Baker)

Feature Films; Producer (with Peter Lord and David Sproxton)

Chicken Run, 2000 (director and author of story with Peter Lord)
Wallace & Gromit: The Curse of the Were-Rabbit, 2005 (director with Steve Box; author with Steve Box, Bob Baker, and Mark Burton)

HONORS AND AWARDS

BAFTA Award (British Academy of Film and Television Arts): 1990, best short animated film, for *A Grand Day Out;* 1994, best short animated film, for *The Wrong Trousers;* 1997, best short animated film, for *A Close Shave;* 2006, Alexander Korda Award for outstanding British film of the year, for *Wallace & Gromit: The Curse of the Were-Rabbit*
Academy Award (Academy of Motion Picture Arts and Sciences): 1991, best short animated film, for *Creature Comforts;* 1994, best short animated film, for *The Wrong Trousers;* 1997, best short animated film, for *A Close Shave;* 2006, best animated feature film, for *Wallace & Gromit: The Curse of the Were-Rabbit*
Commander of the British Empire: 1997
National Board of Review Award: 2001, best animated film, for *Chicken Run*
Broadcast Film Critics Association Award: 2001, best animated film, for *Chicken Run*
Golden Satellite Award (International Press Academy): 2001, best motion picture, animated or mixed media, for *Chicken Run*
British Animation Award: 2002, best European feature film, for *Chicken Run*
Annie Awards (International Animated Film Society): 2006 (four awards), best animated feature, best character design in an animated feature, best directing in an animated feature, and best writing in an animated feature, for *Wallace & Gromit: The Curse of the Were-Rabbit*

FURTHER READING

Books

Authors and Artists for Young Adults, Vol. 32, 2000

Boorman, John, and Walter Donahue, editors. *Projections 5: Filmmakers on Filmmaking,* 1996

Contemporary Theatre, Film, and Television, Vol. 33, 2001

Grant, John. *Masters of Animation,* 2001

International Dictionary of Films and Filmmakers, Volume 4: *Writers and Production Artists,* 2000

Something about the Author, Vol. 113, 2000

Periodicals

Animation Magazine, June 2000, p.10

Entertainment Weekly, June 23, 2000, p.58; Oct. 7, 2005, p.43

Film Journal International, July 2005, p.76

Guardian (London), June 2, 2000, p.8

Independent (London), Apr. 4, 1994, p.18; Mar. 10, 1996, p.2; Nov. 22, 1997, p.22

New York Times, Dec. 1, 1996, sec. 6, p.110; Apr. 30, 2000, sec. 2A, p.27; Sep. 11, 2005, sec. 2, p.48

People, July 24, 2000, p.135

Print, May/June 1997, p.86

Washington Post, Mar. 19, 1995, p.Y7

Online Articles

http://news.bbc.co.uk/1/hi/entertainment/film/4309544.stm (BBC News, "Gromit Film 'A Force of Britishness,'" Oct. 9, 2005)

http://www.bfi.org.uk/features/interviews/harryhausenpark.html (British Film Institute, "Ray Harryhausen and Nick Park," Nov. 22, 2003)

http://filmforce.ign.com/articles/655/655696p1.html (IGN Entertainment, "Interview: Nick Park," Oct. 4, 2005)

http://www.museum.tv/archives/etv/P/htmlP/parknick/parknick.htm (Museum of Broadcast Communications, "Encyclopedia of Television 1st edition: Nick Park," 1997)

http://www.premiere.com/article.asp?section_id=6&article_id=2264 (Premiere Magazine, "Nick Park: Our Exclusive Interview," 2005)

Online Databases

Biography Resource Center Online, 2006, articles from *Authors and Artists for Young Adults,* 2000; *Contemporary Authors Online,* 2006; *Contemporary Theatre, Film, and Television,* 2001

ADDRESS

Nick Park
Aardman Animations, Ltd.
Gas Ferry Road
Bristol BS1 6UN
England

WORLD WIDE WEB SITES

http://www.aardman.com
http://www.wallaceandgromitfoundation.org

Ben Roethlisberger 1982-

American Professional Football Player with the Pittsburgh Steelers
Youngest Quarterback Ever to Win the Super Bowl

BIRTH

Ben Roethlisberger (pronounced ROTH-liss-bur-ger) was born on March 2, 1982, in Lima, Ohio. He was the only child of Ken Roethlisberger, an auto executive, and Ida Roethlisberger. They divorced when Ben was only two years old; six years later, his mother was killed in an automobile accident. By that time his father had re-married, and he and his wife Brenda provided

Ben with a loving environment to overcome this tragedy. They also gave Ben a younger sister, Carlee.

YOUTH

Roethlisberger grew up in Findlay, Ohio, a blue-collar town 90 miles northwest of the state capital of Columbus. Overcoming the loss of his mother, who died when he was only about eight years old, was a painful challenge for young Ben. "You go through a lot of things, especially at that young of [an] age," he recalled. "That's why I think my dad and I are so close. It was always him and I. That's the thing I was truly blessed with, to have someone like my dad there for me and with me through it all." Ken Roethlisberger also instilled in his son the values of hard work and humility, which he demonstrated on the sports field. Young Ben seemed to have a natural aptitude for athletics, excelling even while in grade school. He played sports from a young age, mostly basketball and football.

“

"You go through a lot of things, especially at that young of [an] age," Roethlisberger said about his mother's death. "That's why I think my dad and I are so close. It was always him and I. That's the thing I was truly blessed with, to have someone like my dad there for me and with me through it all."

EDUCATION

Roethlisberger attended Findlay High School, playing both basketball and football. As a freshman and sophomore, he played quarterback for the school's junior varsity team. As a junior, he moved up to the varsity football team, playing wide receiver. He was tall but thin, so he gave way to the starting quarterback—the coach's son, who was a senior. According to the coach, "there was no controversy about it at the time. For Ben, it was all about basketball back then. He was never even going to play college football." Because of the position switch, Roethlisberger didn't get much interest in his quarterbacking talents from major college programs. Between his junior and senior years, he attended a camp at Miami University in Oxford, Ohio. Miami's coach, Terry Hoeppner, was impressed with his skills but wasn't ready to extend him a scholarship offer. "I didn't want to be the genius to offer this guy who never played quarterback a scholarship," the coach said. When the senior threw six touchdowns in his first high school game, Hoeppner recalled, "I said, 'That's good enough for me.'"

Roethlisberger went on to have an outstanding senior year as Findlay's quarterback. He led the team to a 10-2 record that year, taking them to the second round of the Ohio state playoffs. The ten wins included a last-minute victory in which his team trailed by four points with only 33 seconds left. He set state records by throwing for 4,041 yards and 54 touchdowns. For his senior year performance in 1999, he was named the state's Division I Offensive Player of the Year. By that time major college programs, including Ohio State University, had come calling. Roethlisberger was concerned about playing time, however, and he thought at Miami University of Ohio, a member of the Mid-American Conference (MAC), he might have a chance to be a four-year starter. He connected with Coach Hoeppner, whom he now considers a "second father" to him. In December he signed a letter of intent to attend Miami; he spent the rest of his senior year captaining Findlay's basketball and baseball teams. He played point guard for the basketball team and shortstop for the baseball team, and was named to all-league and all-district teams in both sports. He also set Findlay's scoring record in basketball, shooting 1,095 points during his three-year varsity career.

After graduating from Findlay High, Roethlisberger entered Miami University in the fall of 2000. He majored in physical education as he concentrated on improving his football skills. After attending Miami for four years, Roethlisberger decided to leave school for the National Football League. Only four credit hours shy of his degree, he plans to finish his university schooling sometime in the future.

CAREER HIGHLIGHTS

College—The Miami (Ohio) University RedHawks

At Miami, Roethlisberger sat out his first year while senior quarterback Mike Bath led the RedHawks. By taking this "redshirt" season, he could practice with the team without using any of his four years of athletic eligibility. In 2001 he won the starting quarterback position and opened the season with two losses against Michigan and Iowa, two teams from the powerful Big Ten Conference. At home against cross-state rival Cincinnati, however, Roethlisberger completed 20 of 25 passes for 264 yards and two touchdowns in a 21-14 victory. He led the team on a seven-game winning streak before finishing the year 7-5. This included a last-second victory over Akron that inspired the quarterback's nickname. The 70-yard "Hail Mary" touchdown pass that won the game was called "Big Ben," and the name soon stuck to the 6'5" quarterback. Roethlisberger set several Miami single-season records in 2001, with 241 completions for 3,105 yards and 25

In 2003, Roethlisberger's last season with Miami of Ohio, the RedHawks won 13 straight games, including their first MAC Championship. Here, Big Ben (left) sets up for a pass as teammate Mike Smith (right) fakes a handoff.

touchdowns. As a result, he was named Mid-American Conference Freshman of the Year and a member of All-MAC second team. In addition, he was named to the Freshman All-America Team by the Football Writers' Association of America.

Roethlisberger has said that it was his second season in which he started feeling comfortable with Miami's offensive system. He also bulked up physically, going from 210 pounds to 240. In 2002, he led the team to another winning season, as the RedHawks again finished 7-5. He completed 271 of 428 passing attempts for 3,238 yards and 22 touchdowns, posting new school records in each of those categories. He made honorable mention on the NFL Draft Report's All-American team and was second-team All-MAC behind Marshall's Byron Leftwich, a future NFL star for the Jacksonville Jaguars.

Nevertheless, Roethlisberger wanted more than anything to win a championship at Miami. He faced the pressure of being ranked as one of the top 25 players in the nation—the *Sporting News* named him their top quarterback—and he responded. He started the 2003 season with an opening loss against Iowa, in which he threw for 250 yards but also four interceptions. But after that, the quarterback led his team to a dream season. The RedHawks won 13 straight games, including their first MAC Championship game, a decisive 49-27 victory over Bowling Green. With a 49-28 victory over Louisville in the GMAC Bowl, Miami finished the 2003 season with a No. 14 ranking in the Associated Press (AP) national poll, their highest ranking since 1975. Roethlisberger rewrote Miami's single-season records yet again, completing 342 of 495 passes (69.1%) for 4,486 yards and 37 touchdowns, as well as gaining 4,597 yards in total offense. His Miami offense also set MAC records for season scoring (553 points) and total offense (7,016 yards). He was named one of the ten semifinalists for the Davey O'Brien Award, given each year to the top college quarterback of the year, and finished ninth in the voting for the Heisman Trophy, awarded to the best player in college football.

"I'd say I got my feet wet, but I got my whole leg wet," Roethlisberger said about his first game as a rookie. "It's tough, you come out and your first game is against probably one of, if not the best, defense in the NFL."

Having accomplished a conference title, bowl-game victory, and a final ranking in the Top 15, Roethlisberger decided to leave Miami even though he had one year of eligibility left. After three years as a starter, he owned most of the school's career passing records, including 1,304 passing attempts, 65.5% pass completion percentage, 84 touchdowns, and 10,829 total passing yards. The mobile quarterback, who ran for seven touchdowns during his college career, also held the school's record for total offense, with 11,075 yards. He entered the 2004 NFL Draft as the Mid-American Conference Offensive Player of the Year, a third-team selection on the Associated Press's All-America list, and an NFL Draft Report first-team All-American. The Pittsburgh Steelers selected him in the first round, making him the 11th player drafted overall. He signed a six-year contract that paid him $14 million, plus an $8 million roster bonus.

NFL — The Pittsburgh Steelers

Roethlisberger holds up a Pittsburgh Steelers jersey after being selected 11th overall in the first round of the 2004 NFL draft.

When the Steelers drafted Roethlisberger in 2004, they had intended to give him time to learn their offensive system. Professional football is a much faster and more complex game than college football, and quarterback is the most demanding position. Roethlisberger was to be the third quarterback on Pittsburgh's roster, but a season-ending injury to backup Charlie Batch during training camp moved him up the depth chart. Then, during the second game of the season, against the Baltimore Ravens, starting quarterback Tommy Maddox went down with an elbow injury. Roethlisberger entered his first NFL game with his team losing in the third quarter, 20-0. Although he threw two touchdowns, he also gave up two interceptions, including one returned for a Baltimore touchdown. Pittsburgh lost the game 30-13, but the rookie quarterback was unfazed by the loss. "I'd say I got my feet wet, but I got my whole leg wet," Roethlisberger said. "It's tough, you come out and your first game is against probably one of, if not the best, defense in the NFL."

Maddox's injury was severe enough to keep him out of the lineup, so the next week Roethlisberger made his first NFL start against the Miami Dolphins. Facing wet weather, Steelers head coach Bill Cowher kept the game plan simple; Roethlisberger only made 22 passing attempts, completing 12 of them with one touchdown and one interception. Pittsburgh's defense held Miami to a single field goal and the rookie quarterback led the offense on a game-clinching touchdown drive in fourth quarter as the Steelers won 13-3. The next week against the Cincinnati Bengals, Roethlisberger completed 17 of 25 passes with no interceptions, leading the offense to the go-ahead touchdown in the fourth quarter in the Steelers' 28-17 victory. In Big Ben's third start, his mobility helped him elude the Cleveland Browns' defense. He not only went 16-for-21 for 231 yards and one touchdown, he rushed for another Pittsburgh score en route to a 34-23 victory.

NFL fans and teams were noticing Roethlisberger's fast start. His ability to stand in the pocket and deliver the ball quickly, yet scramble away from trouble when necessary, led some to compare him to Hall-of-Famer Dan Marino of the Miami Dolphins, the NFL's all-time passing leader. In his next two games, Roethlisberger went 39-of-49 in a comeback 24-20 victory over the Dallas Cowboys and a decisive 34-20 win over the defending Super Bowl champs, the New England Patriots. The latter performance led Cowher to name Roethlisberger Pittsburgh's permanent starting quarterback. The following week the rookie threw two touchdowns in a 27-3 win over the previously unbeaten Philadelphia Eagles, stretching his record as starter to 6-0 and earning him honors as AFC Offensive Rookie of the Month. Roethlisberger didn't light up the scoreboard in his next three games, but even though his production was low, Pittsburgh's league-leading defense made up for it and the Steelers extended their winning streak to 9-0. The nine wins also tied Roethlisberger for most wins by an NFL rookie. As he continued winning, the city of Pittsburgh went wild for Big Ben, with local eateries naming sandwiches after him and sales of his No. 7 jersey skyrocketing.

"I told someone, 'If I'm dreaming, I don't want to wake up because I want to keep this going.' What's so special about this team is everyone is selfless."

If Roethlisberger had any doubters, they were silenced by his performance in week 13 of the season against the Jacksonville Jaguars. Down by two points with less than two minutes left, the quarterback led his team to score the game-winning field goal. He finished 14-for-17 for 221 yards, two touchdowns, and a near-perfect passer rating of 158. (In the NFL, this rating is calculated using completion percentage and yards, touchdowns, and interceptions per attempt, with 158.3 being a perfect score.) His poise helped rally the Steelers over the New York Giants in week 15, and his toughness helped Pittsburgh clinch home-field advantage throughout the playoffs the following week, when he played despite enduring a rough hit to the ribs while throwing a touchdown pass against Baltimore. Roethlisberger left that game in the fourth quarter, and Tommy Maddox started Pittsburgh's final game of the season, a victory over the Buffalo Bills. Although he didn't play in this last game, Roethlisberger was thrilled with

Roethlisberger drops back to pass during a game against the Jacksonville Jaguars in December 2004.

Pittsburgh's 15-1 season: "I told someone, 'If I'm dreaming, I don't want to wake up because I want to keep this going.' What's so special about this team is everyone is selfless."

A Rookie in the Playoffs

There was no question Roethlisberger would lead the Steelers into the playoffs, especially since he had two weeks to heal before their first game, against the New York Jets. At first, the rookie seemed affected by the pressure: he gave up an interception that was returned by the Jets for a touchdown. After leading the Steelers to tie the score, a second Roethlisberger interception gave the Jets the chance to win the game with a field goal. A Jets miss led to overtime, and Big Ben took his team from their own 13-yard line to kick their own game-winner. Despite the 20-17 victory, the quarterback knew he hadn't performed his best. "I did everything I could to lose the game," he said. "I've got to play better. That was terrible. The game we played today is not going to cut it."

> *"When there are doubters, it always fuels the fire a little bit," Roethlisberger commented. "When people say you can't do something, if you are a competitor, that drives you. I think there probably is a little chip on my shoulder. But that's not the whole drive. Wanting to be the best and wanting to win, they push me, too."*

The Steelers had home field for the AFC title game the following week, a rematch against New England. Roethlisberger hoped to become the first rookie quarterback to lead his team to the Super Bowl, but the defending champs had a game plan that put pressure on Big Ben. He threw three interceptions, including one returned for a touchdown that gave the Patriots a 24-3 lead. Although Roethlisberger later threw two touchdowns, it wasn't enough and the Steelers lost the game 41-27. The young quarterback tried to be philosophical after the loss: "It wasn't a great game on my part, but I learned an awful lot this season. We had a great season, but there are a lot of people—some in that locker room—that now think [it's a disappointment]."

Roethlisberger's talent, determination, and modesty had made him the toast of Pittsburgh during his first NFL season. Although his sub-par performance in the playoffs brought him some criticism, there was no denying the quarterback had enjoyed an incredible rookie season. His 13 wins as a starter set a record for most wins by a rookie quarterback and also made him the first NFL quarterback ever to achieve a 13-0 regular season record. He broke Dan Marino's records for highest rookie quarterback passer rating (98.1) and highest rookie quarterback completion percentage (66.4%), both of which were also Pittsburgh team records. The Associated Press named him their Offensive Rookie of the Year, while the *Sporting News* accorded him Rookie of the Year honors. When the NFL voted on their Rookie of the Year Award, Roethlisberger was their unanimous selection. His success also earned him some $4.5 million in endorsement deals his first year.

A Super Season

When Pittsburgh opened the 2005 season, Roethlisberger was determined to take his team to the next level. Part of it was to prove himself against naysayers who gave most of the credit for the Steelers' great season to their outstanding running backs and No. 1 ranked defense: "When there are doubters, it always fuels the fire a little bit," the athlete commented. "When people say you can't do something, if you are a competitor, that drives you. I think there probably is a little chip on my shoulder. But that's not the whole drive. Wanting to be the best and wanting to win, they push me, too." Still, he recognized it would be difficult to duplicate the team's success of 2004. "The bottom line is that I can have a better season [statistically] and we could still win fewer games than we did a year ago. What matters is that we win the ones that count."

In the Steelers' season opener against the Tennessee Titans, Roethlisberger made his statistics count: 9-of-11 for 211 yards and two touchdowns, for a perfect passer rating of 158.3. Combined with a record-breaking day by running back Willie Parker, the Steelers won 34-7. The quarterback shook off a sore knee to lead Pittsburgh to a 27-7 win over the Houston Texans to extend his regular season victory streak to 15. In a rematch against Super Bowl champ New England, however, Roethlisberger experienced his first regular-season loss as a starter, although he did complete an 85-yard touchdown pass to Hines Ward. Big Ben returned the team to their winning ways in their next game against the San Diego Chargers, but suffered a knee injury on the game-winning drive. Roethlisberger sat out the next game, a loss to Jacksonville, but returned to throw two touchdowns the following week in a 27-13 victory over Cincinnati. He then threw two more scores in a close 20-19 victory over Baltimore, but reinjured his knee during the game.

Roethlisberger's injury, a slight tear in the cartilage that stabilizes the knee, was enough to require arthroscopic surgery. He missed three more games, during which Pittsburgh raised their record to 7-3. He returned for a Monday night game against the undefeated Indianapolis Colts, but suffered two interceptions and three sacks as the Colts defense smothered Pittsburgh, 26-7. With a loss to division rival Cincinnati the next week, the 7-5 Steelers were in danger of missing the playoffs. Roethlisberger set to work: despite a sprained thumb on his throwing hand, he led the Steelers to four straight victories. Over the four games he completed 60% of his passes, threw only two interceptions (neither led to opponent scores), and rushed for the game's only touchdown in an 18-3 victory over the Chicago Bears. The Steelers finished the season 11-5, earning the last AFC spot in the playoffs.

Receiver Hines Ward called Big Ben "the catalyst of our whole offense. The quarterback has to have confidence, or how else will the rest of the 10 guys follow him? He's going out there confident and having trust in his teammates to make plays."

Winning On and Off the Field

The Steelers had a tough road to the Super Bowl: being seeded sixth in the AFC meant they would have to play all their games on the road. Their first game was against Cincinnati, with whom they had split two games during the regular season. Bengals quarterback Carson Palmer went out with an injury on the first play, but Cincinnati still led 10-0 after the first quarter. Roethlisberger brought the team back to win 31-17, going 14-of-19 for 208 yards with three touchdowns. The next week brought a rematch with Indianapolis; although Roethlisberger threw two touchdowns, Pittsburgh fans will forever remember it for "The Tackle." The Steelers had the ball near the Indianapolis goal line with 80 seconds left in the game and a three-point lead. They only had to hang on to the ball to win the game, but usually sure-handed running back Jerome Bettis fumbled. Colts defensive back Nick Harper picked up the ball and looked like he would run it back for the winning touchdown. Instead, Roethlisberger ran back, twisted his body, and made a one-handed tackle of Harper. The defense then limited the Colts to a field goal attempt, which was no good. The Steelers won 21-18, becoming the first No. 6 seed to go to a conference championship.

Playing against the Denver Broncos at their home stadium in the AFC title game, Roethlisberger directed the Steelers offense to a quick lead, including a 101-second touchdown drive just before halftime that made it 24-3. He finished the game 21-of-29 for 275 yards, two touchdowns, and no intercep-

Roethlisberger (# 7) and Nick Harper (# 25) of the Indianapolis Colts, in the play that became known to Pittsburgh fans as "The Tackle." Big Ben prevented a touchdown, and the Steelers won 21-18.

tions. He also scored the game's last touchdown on a four-yard run, making the final score 34-17. Pittsburgh was going to the Super Bowl, the first team ever to beat the top three seeds in the playoffs. Although Roethlisberger was the first to credit the play of his teammates, receiver Hines Ward noted that Big Ben was "the catalyst of our whole offense. The quarterback has to have confidence, or how else will the rest of the 10 guys follow him? He's going out there confident and having trust in his teammates to make plays."

At the age of 23, Roethlisberger was about to lead his team in one of the most high-pressure situations in all of sports: the Super Bowl, where the Steelers would face the Seattle Seahawks. At first, the Steeler offense looked shaky against Seattle: they failed to make a first down until the second quarter, then on the same drive Roethlisberger threw an interception. On Pittsburgh's next possession, however, the quarterback converted a crucial third down-and-28 with a pass to the game's eventual Most Valuable Player, Hines Ward. Roethlisberger capped the drive with a one-yard touchdown run that barely crossed the goal line. That gave Pittsburgh the lead, 7-3, and the Steelers never looked back. Although he threw a second interception that led to a Seahawks touchdown, the team held on to win 21-10.

Roethlisberger's passer rating of 22.6—he was 9-of-23 for 123 yards, no touchdowns, and two interceptions—was the lowest ever by a winning Super Bowl quarterback. But what the statistics didn't show were the little things he did to help his team: escaping sacks, scrambling for first downs to keep drives alive, and throwing a key block on the trick pass play from Antwaan Randle El to Ward that scored Pittsburgh's last touchdown. As usual, Big Ben was forthright in assessing his game: "When you think about the Super Bowl, you imagine yourself coming out and playing your best football, and it wasn't that way." He credited his teammates for the victory, noting: "They're not my supporting cast—I'm their supporting cast." Despite a less-than-ideal performance, however, Roethlisberger had become the youngest quarterback ever to lead his team to a Super Bowl victory. "A lot of people say you can't do it, they doubt you, they disbelieve, and it shows anything can be done."

"

"When you think about the Super Bowl, you imagine yourself coming out and playing your best football, and it wasn't that way," Roethlisberger said about his performance. He credited his teammates for the victory: "They're not my supporting cast—I'm their supporting cast."

With all his success on the football field, Roethlisberger is determined to give back to the community off the field. He has gotten involved in charities on both the national and local level. After the horrific tsunami that hit Asia in December 2004, Roethlisberger donated his first playoff game paycheck, worth $18,000, to the relief effort. He has also donated his time, appearing at fundraisers and visiting children in the hospital. "Young people with special needs and without special needs need to have someone give them hope," he said. "If my position with the Steelers makes me a role model to young people, I want to demonstrate to others that everybody deserves respect and compassion." While victories on the football field excite the fans, Roethlisberger would rather touch people's lives by inspiring them to help others. "When I'm done playing football," he noted, "I would like people to say, 'Not only was Ben a good quarterback, most of all he was a good guy who thought of others before himself.' I consider myself a passionate person and I want to share that."

HOME AND FAMILY

Roethlisberger owns a townhouse near the Pittsburgh Steelers' practice facilities. He is single, but lives with his dog Zeus, a Rottweiler. He keeps in close contact with his parents, who attend all Steelers games and stay with him on home-game weekends.

HOBBIES AND OTHER INTERESTS

Roethlisberger still enjoys basketball and has also taken up golf and fishing. He is a movie fan, citing action movies like *Gladiator* and *Bad Boys* as his favorites. He also enjoys playing video games and watching pro wrestling. During the off-season, he likes to spend time riding his motorcycles. In June 2006 his hobby caused controversy when he was injured in a collision with an automobile. Roethlisberger was not wearing a helmet (which is legal in Pennsylvania) and fractured his nose, upper and lower jaws, and facial bones. His injuries, which also included two lost teeth and a mild concussion, required seven hours of surgery to repair. Doctors felt confident that he could recover in time for the 2006 regular football season, so Big Ben was lucky. According to the National Highway Traffic Safety Administration, an unhelmeted motorcycle rider in a crash is 40 percent more likely to suffer a fatal head injury and 15 percent more likely to suffer a nonfatal injury than a rider wearing a helmet.

"When I'm done playing football," Roethlisberger noted, "I would like people to say, 'Not only was Ben a good quarterback, most of all he was a good guy who thought of others before himself.' I consider myself a passionate person and I want to share that."

HONORS AND AWARDS

Named First Team Freshman All-American (Football Writers Association of America): 2001
Named First Team All-American (NFL Draft Report): 2003

Pepsi Rookie of the Year Award (National Football League): 2004
NFL Rookie of the Year Award (*Sporting News*): 2004
NFL Offensive Rookie of the Year Award (Associated Press): 2004

FURTHER READING

Books

Roethlisberger: Pittsburgh's Own Big Ben, 2004

Periodicals

Detroit Free Press, Feb. 6, 2006, Sports section, p.4
Exceptional Parent, Sep. 2005, p.16
Forbes, July 4, 2005, p.138
New York Times, Sep. 9, 2005, p.D3; Nov. 28, 2005, p.D1; Jan. 22, 2006, sec. 8, p.1
Philadelphia Daily News, Feb. 6, 2006, p.108
Pittsburgh Post-Gazette, Jan. 29, 2006; June 14, 2006
San Jose Mercury-News, Feb. 3, 2006, p.C1
Sporting News, Sep. 15, 2003, p.14; Nov. 22, 2004, p.16
Sports Illustrated, Oct. 25, 2004, p.31; Nov. 8, 2004, p.54; Sep. 5, 2005, p.92
Sports Illustrated for Kids, Sep. 1, 2005, p.30
Time, Jan. 10, 2005, p.58
USA Today, Jan.12, 2005, p.C1; Feb. 3, 2006, p.E1

Online Articles

http://www.nfl.com/gamecenter/recap/NFL_20040919_PIT@BAL (NFL.com, "Ravens Run Past Steelers, 30-13," Sep. 19, 2004)
http://www.nfl.com/gamecenter/recap/NFL_20050102_PIT@BUF (NFL.com, "Steelers' Backups Bop Bills 29-24," Jan. 2, 2005)
http://www.nfl.com/gamecenter/recap/NFL_20050115_NYJ@PIT (NFL.com, "Struggling Steelers Stave off Jets in OT," Jan. 15, 2005)
http://www.nfl.com/gamecenter/recap/NFL_20050123_NE@PIT (NFL.com, "Patriots Rout Steelers in AFC Title Game," Jan. 23, 2005)
http://www.nfl.com/gamecenter/recap/NFL_20060122_PIT@DEN (NFL.com, "Steelers Super Bowl Bound with 34-17 Win," Jan. 22, 2006)
http://www.superbowl.com/gamecenter/recap/NFL_20060205_SEA@PIT (NFL.com, "Steelers Capture Super Bowl XL Title, 21-10," Feb. 5, 2006)

Online Databases

Biography Resource Center Online, 2005

ADDRESS

Ben Roethlisberger
Pittsburgh Steelers
P.O. Box 6763
Pittsburgh, PA 15212

WORLD WIDE WEB SITES

http://www.steelers.com
http://www.bigben7.com
http://www.nfl.com
http://www.nflplayers.com

BRIEF ENTRY

Jamie Lynn Spears 1991-

American Actress
Star of the Hit Nickelodeon TV Series "Zoey 101"

EARLY YEARS

Jamie Lynn Marie Spears was born on April 4, 1991, in McComb, Mississippi, a town that is only a few miles from her family's home in Kentwood, Louisiana. Her father, Jamie, worked as a building contactor, and her mother, Lynne, was an elementary school teacher. Jamie Lynn has an older sister, Britney, and an older brother, Bryan.

When Jamie Lynn was born, Britney was 10 years old and already an aspiring singer and actress. (For more information on Britney see *Biography Today,* Jan. 2001.) Their parents encouraged their oldest daughter to pursue her dreams and were willing to make big sacrifices to see Britney succeed in the entertainment business. A few months after Jamie Lynn was born, she moved to New York City with her sister and her mother Lynne to further Britney's singing and acting career, while father Jamie and brother Bryan remained in Kentwood. In New York City, Britney attended the Professional Performing Arts School for three summers, appeared in television commercials, and acted in off-Broadway plays. In 1992 Britney landed a role on "The Mickey Mouse Club," which filmed in Orlando, Florida, and the entire family moved there for two years until the series was cancelled. They moved back to Kentwood in 1993.

When Jamie Lynn was only six years old, Britney signed a recording contract with Jive Records and had to leave home to record her first album, *Baby One More Time,* which was completed in 1999. It turned out to be an overwhelming success, and Jamie Lynn got to see her sister become a superstar. She also accompanied her sister on several concert and television appearances. It was difficult to see her big sister leave home at such an early age. Jamie Lynn loved being the baby of the family, but it was hard too. "The best thing is they all spoil me," she said recently. "Then it kind of sucks 'cause I don't have anybody at home. I'm the only kid." Jamie Lynn tried acting herself, trying out for several school plays. "My only part in a school play was as an extra orphan in *Annie* at age nine," she recalled. "I was never the lead. I was pretty shy." However, she realized that she wanted to act and sing, and her parents encouraged her to audition for local plays and television commercials.

Jamie Lynn loved being the baby of the family, but it was hard too. "The best thing is they all spoil me," she said recently. "Then it kind of sucks 'cause I don't have anybody at home. I'm the only kid."

MAJOR ACCOMPLISHMENTS

In 2002 Spears got her first job in the entertainment business. She made a brief appearance in *Crossroads,* a film that starred her older sister, Britney. "It was cool doing it with Britney because she could really help me—although, I didn't get to say anything in the movie!" Jamie Lynn said in a re-

Jamie Lynn and the cast of "All That."

cent interview. "But it was fun being in front of the camera. And it'd be fun to work with my sister again." She also appeared in the MTV documentary "Driven," which focused on Britney's climb to the top of the music charts. During the show, Jamie Lynn performed a rap number with her brother, Bryan.

When Nickelodeon executives saw her sing and dance, they invited her to audition for their hit show "All That," a comedy sketch show performed by kids for kids. It was quite an opportunity for Jamie Lynn, because "All That" is the same show that launched the careers of other young stars, including Amanda Bynes and Kenan Thompson. In her audition, Jamie Lynn did a funny impression of an 84-year-old bouncer named Thelma Stump, who throws people out of windows and attacks them with leaf blowers—a character she based on her own grandmother.

Joining the Cast of "All That"

Nick executives loved what they saw, and in 2002 they invited Jamie Lynn to join the cast of "All That." "Based on her audition, I would have added her to the cast of 'All That' even if she had not been a Spears," asserted the producer of the show, Dan Schneider. "I see the same drive in her as in Britney," claims Virgil Fabian, the director of "All That" who had also directed Britney on "The Mickey Mouse Club" in the early 1990s. Britney also saw a special quality in her sister. "Of course I'm biased, but I definitely think Jamie Lynn has the 'It' quality," Britney asserted. "She shines, and I'm proud of her."

Jamie Lynn was thrilled to join the hit show, but she was also nervous. "At first I was too scared to act in front of these people, so I was real shy," she remembered. "But then, they were actually really nice. I thought they were going to be these serious people. But they were a lot of fun." It wasn't long before Jamie joined right into the silliness of the show—she was tossed into trash bins and doused with water and egg yolks, and she performed funny impressions in front of a studio audience. Her castmates were impressed with her attitude. "I was expecting someone who was going to be a little kiddish, kind of immature," said Shane Lyons, a fellow cast member on "All That." "But what we got was someone who could relate and talk and just mess around with us on our level." Fellow cast member Chelsea Brummet agreed. "Jamie has the maturity level of, like, a 15-year-old, which is awesome." Others thought that because her sister is a superstar, Jamie Lynn might be stuck up. "I thought she'd have a limo and bodyguards," revealed castmate Lisa Foiles, "but she's totally cool."

Some cast members on "All That" thought that because her sister is a superstar, Jamie Lynn might be stuck up. "I thought she'd have a limo and bodyguards," revealed castmate Lisa Foiles, "but she's totally cool."

”

"Zoey 101"

Jamie Lynn became a success with her role on "All That." After two years on the popular show, she met with the producer, Dan Schneider, who offered her her own series on Nick. "It was a total blessing," she remembered. "When they told me, I started screaming and called all my friends. I was even more excited than with 'All That' because it was my very own show."

Schneider created "Zoey 101" especially for Jamie Lynn. Her character, Zoey Brooks, is a 13-year-old girl who is one of the first females to enroll in an all-male school, the Pacific Coast Academy. "She's a lot like me," said Jamie Lynn. "It's a lot of fun. I get to go to work and be myself all day." Jamie Lynn has pointed out both similarities and differences between her and the character of Zoey. "I could never try out for the all-boys basketball team like she did!" she said in an interview. "She's probably more assertive than I am. Like, she does a lot of things I'd never think of doing, like going to a boarding school. I just could never be away from home for that long—I'm so close with my family."

Jamie Lynn also got to work with her sister, Britney, to record the theme song of the show. Britney co-wrote the song and coached her sister in the studio. "She totally helped me out in the studio," Jamie Lynn recalled. "She'd say, 'Stop being nervous, you have a great voice.'" When people have compared her to her famous older sister, Jamie Lynn is flattered. "It's hard," she admitted in an interview. "But Britney is pretty great, so it's the biggest compliment I could get. I never look at it as a bad thing." Britney's celebrity has taught her younger sister a few valuable lessons. "I've learned to stay close with my family as she has and that it's really hard work in show business," Jamie Lynn revealed. "I've also learned to not listen to all of the gossip. I guess people don't really realize that less than half that stuff is really true."

Jamie Lynn has pointed out both similarities and differences between her and the character of Zoey. "I could never try out for the all-boys basketball team like she did!" she said in an interview. "She's probably more assertive than I am. Like, she does a lot of things I'd never think of doing, like going to a boarding school. I just could never be away from home for that long—I'm so close with my family."

"Zoey 101" quickly became one of the most popular shows on Nickelodeon. To capitalize on the show's success, Nick released a soundtrack of "Zoey 101," a book series, and a clothing line. At the Nickelodeon's Kids Choice Awards in 2006, Jamie Lynn won the award for Favorite TV Actress. She has been featured on the covers of several magazines, including *American Cheerleader* and *Seventeen.* Although she is now recognized as a star in her own right, Jamie Lynn has tried to stay grounded. "I wouldn't say I'm a celebrity, but the best thing is just being able to go to work every day and do something I love," she said. "I'm just one of those people that doesn't want to be noticed or anything."

Jamie Lynn does lend her celebrity to raise money for worthy causes. She filmed a public service announcement to help raise funds for the victims of the tsunami in Indonesia, has been active in raising money for the victims

"Zoey 101" has been so successful that it produced a book series, a DVD collection, a CD music mix soundtrack, and even a clothing line.

of Hurricane Katrina, and has volunteered with the American Red Cross. Despite her busy schedule, Jamie Lynn has said that she will always find time to volunteer and help raise money for people in need. "I think that, out of everything I do, helping other people is the most important thing you can do," she asserted. "There's always time for that!"

Education

Jamie Lynn attends Parklane Academy in McComb, Mississippi. She is outgoing and athletic, playing on both the softball and basketball teams. She is also on her school's cheerleading squad, which was invited to participate in the 2006 National All-Star Cheerleading Championship. Although she is recognized as a celebrity, her schoolmates do not treat her any differently. "I've grown up with these people all my life, so they don't really treat me different," she claimed. "I've taken some of my friends on the set. They get to be extras, so they like it a lot." She has described herself as a serious student. "I'm the more outgoing one between me and my sister Britney, but I like to get my school stuff done because I want good grades. Or try, at least!"

"I have a lot of guy friends, but I don't want a boyfriend or anything," Jamie Lynn claimed. "I'm not allowed to go on a date until I'm 16 anyway."

Jamie Lynn loves growing up in Kentwood. "I know everybody," she declared. "There's nobody in that town I don't know; it's just fun to know everybody and all my friends live, like, five minutes from me." Jamie Lynn is away in Los Angeles a couple of months out of the year filming "Zoey 101" and also has to travel for business. "I like it a lot but, when you're away from home, you're always going to get a little homesick," she said in an interview. "At the most, I'm away for about three months at a time. The good part is that my friends come out and visit for a week, which is awesome." Those friends don't include a boyfriend, at least not yet. "I have a lot of guy friends, but I don't want a boyfriend or anything," she claimed. "I'm not allowed to go on a date until I'm 16 anyway."

Future Plans

Jamie Lynn has talked about starting a singing career, like her sister, Britney. For the past few years, she has concentrated on her acting career and her hit series "Zoey 101," as well as her classes, cheerleading, and softball. "I'm just focusing on 'Zoey' right now, but I'd like to do movies later," she commented in a recent interview. "I've always said I want to do scary movies, but then I read scripts for funny movies, and I think, 'Oh, I have to do this!' So you never know!"

CREDITS

"All That," 2002-2004
"Zoey 101," 2004-

HONORS AND AWARDS

Kids Choice Award (Nickelodeon): 2006, for Favorite TV Actress

FURTHER READING

Periodicals

Girls' Life, Apr.-May 2005, p.40
New York Post, Apr. 7, 2005, p.86
New York Times, Aug. 7, 2005, p.AR26
Newsweek, Jan. 24, 2005, pp.24, 75
People, Mar. 3, 2003, p.106

ADDRESS

Jamie Lynn Spears
Nickelodeon Studios
231 W. Olive Ave.
Burbank, CA 91502

WORLD WIDE WEB SITES

http://www.jamielynnspears.com
http://www.nick.com

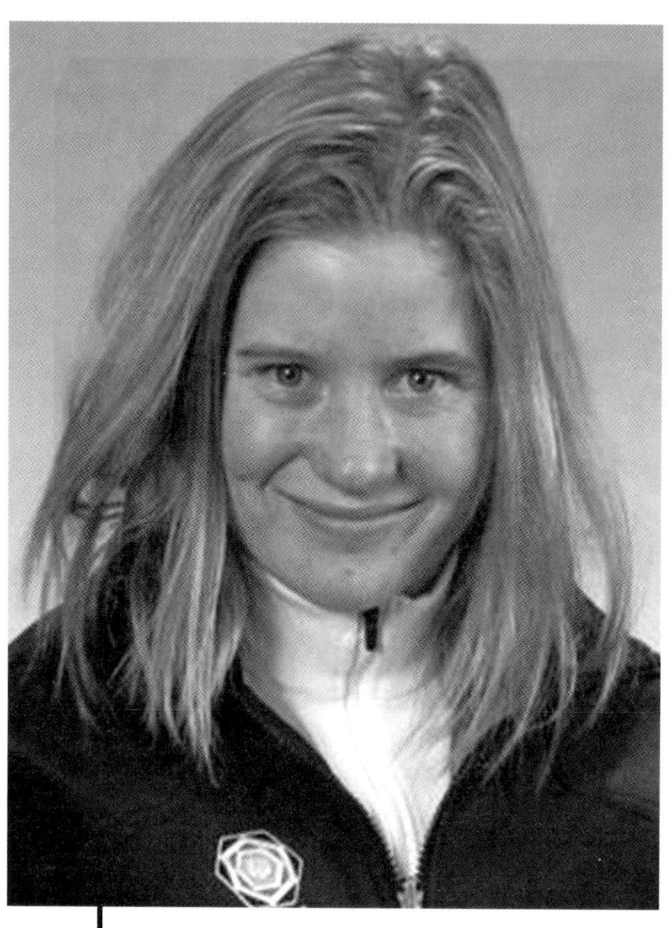

Hannah Teter 1987-

American Professional Snowboarder
Winner of a Gold Medal in the 2006 Winter Olympics

BIRTH

Hannah Teter was born on January 27, 1987, in Belmont, Vermont. Belmont is a tiny town with a population of approximately 328 people. Her father, Jeff Teter, is a construction foreman for the town of Mount Holly, Vermont. Her mother, Patricia (Pat) Teter, is an emergency-room nurse and midwife, a health-care specialist who provides health care for women, especially during pregnancy and childbirth. Pat also heads the town's volunteer rescue squad. According to Teter, her parents were hippies and met at a music festival in Colorado.

Hannah is the youngest of five children and the only girl in the family. Jeff and Pat Teter took all of their kids' names from the Bible. Amen is the oldest brother and works as Teter's manager. Abe and Elijah are members of the United States National Snowboard team and compete on the World Cup circuit. Joshua, the youngest brother, was born with a slight mental handicap. He is developmentally delayed and slightly autistic. Of the five Teter children, only Amen was born in a hospital. The other four were born at home.

YOUTH

Before Teter was born, her parents grew watermelons and cantaloupes on a small family farm in Missouri. They did not have much money, but they were happy. But one year, the summer was extremely hot and the family's well ran dry, so they moved to Vermont to start a new life. Jeff Teter described the move as a spiritual quest.

While Teter was growing up, she was always trying to keep up with her older brothers. The Teters are a close-knit family, so her brothers let her tag along. And she was able to keep up with them. Pat Teter recalled, "She was always right behind them. If they wanted to climb a 50-foot tree, she would be right up there with them, even though she was like four years old. I'd hear her yelling from the treetops, 'Mom! Mom! Look at me! I can make the tree go back and forth!'"

When Abe was 12 years old, he really wanted a trampoline. So he made and sold pies in their neighborhood for $5 each, until he earned enough money to buy one. The Teter kids spent a lot of time bouncing on that trampoline. When Hannah was just four years old, her brothers bounced her off the trampoline and onto a car. As Amen described the incident, "If you bounce right before someone else bounces, it makes them bounce three times as high. So little Hannah would be like four years old out there, bouncing, and one time, they double-bounced her. So you have this little four-year-old girl shot like 15 feet in the air off the trampoline and landing on the roof of the car." Even after that, Teter was not afraid to bounce on the trampoline with her brothers.

The Teter children grew up among skiers and snowboarders. Pat Teter worked at Okemo Mountain Resort, so they were able to ride the ski lifts for free. And Belmont is about an hour away from Stratton, which is the home of the U.S. Open Snowboarding Championships. Teter started snowboarding at the age of eight, following in her brothers' footsteps: "I started watching my four brothers, and especially Elijah, who was boarding when I was really young." Her brothers seemed to be having a lot of fun on their snowboards, so she decided to give it a try. "I was just loving watching them ride, and that's why I started," she recalled. "I wanted to have that kind of fun. And at the same time I was learning a ton of stuff from them, and then I began to go in the small contests that they did."

"

"I started watching my four brothers, and especially Elijah, who was boarding when I was really young," Teter recalled. "I was just loving watching them ride, and that's why I started. I wanted to have that kind of fun. And at the same time I was learning a ton of stuff from them, and then I began to go in the small contests that they did."

"

EDUCATION

By the time Teter reached high school, she was competing regularly. Her competition schedule required her to travel, sometimes in the middle of the week during the school year. When her public high school told her that she was not allowed to miss more than ten days of school, she decided to transfer to Okemo Mountain School, a snowboard academy in Ludlow, Vermont. At Okemo, students snowboard in the morning and take classes in the afternoon. This school also allowed her to miss class time to compete. Teter graduated from Okemo in 2005.

Teter plans to go to college some day. She would like to go to the University of Hawaii because she thinks Hawaii is "the coolest place ever."

CAREER HIGHLIGHTS

Joining Amateur Competitions

Teter began participating in amateur snowboard competitions in 1998. Before long, she was winning these competitions. In 2001, she won the boardercross event at the United States Ski and Snowboard Association (USSA) National Championships. (The USSA is the governing body for U.S. Olympic skiing and snowboarding.) In a boardercross race, groups of four to six snowboarders race down a giant slalom course that has banked turns, jumps, and other features. The first two or three to finish the course move up to the next round.

Teter competing in the semi-finals of the USSA Snowboarding Grand Prix in California, 2004.

In 2002, Teter won the halfpipe event at the Fédération Internationale de Ski (FIS) Junior World Championships. (The FIS is the governing body for international skiing and snowboarding.) The halfpipe competition is the most popular freestyle event, in which the snowboarders perform tricks in a very large snow trough. Riders glide back and forth across a giant U-shaped tube of snow. They gather speed on the downward slope, then perform high-flying aerial tricks at the top of the upward slope. A team of judges evaluates each rider's amplitude (height above the top of the pipe), smoothness (success in linking tricks together), and degree of difficulty, awarding a numerical score. All competitors make qualifying runs, after which the top scorers advance to the finals. The finals consist of more runs, and the top riders earn spots on the podium.

Moving Up to the Professional Level

Later in 2002, Teter began competing at the professional level. At the time, she was at least five years younger than most of her competitors. During her first season as a professional, she won the halfpipe event at two USSA Grand Prix contests and placed second at a Vans Triple Crown competition. At the U.S. Open Snowboarding Championships that year, she placed third in the superpipe event (a larger halfpipe) and slopestyle event (where a succession of riders goes through a series of obstacles, performing tricks along the way). With these two events, she won the overall title and claimed the prize, a brand new Jeep Wrangler. She didn't even have her driver's license yet. "I was in shock," she recalled. "When I got home that night, I was like, 'Whoa, did I just win a car?'"

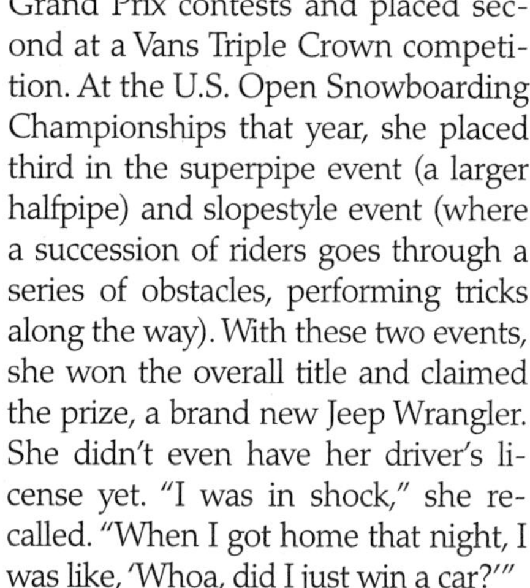

> “
>
> *When Teter won the U.S. Open Snowboarding Championships and won a brand new Jeep Wrangler, she didn't even have her driver's license yet. "I was in shock," she recalled. "When I got home that night, I was like, 'Whoa, did I just win a car?'"*
>
> ”

When she was just 16 years old, Teter became the first woman to land a frontside 900 in competition. This move involves turning two and a half times on the snowboard while up in the air. She has continued to try new and daring moves on her snowboard.

In 2004, the North American Snowsports Journalist Association awarded Teter the Competitor of the Year Award. This was the first time a snowboarder had won this award. Also that year, she was a finalist for the ESPY Awards for Best Female Action Sport Athlete.

Throughout the 2004 and 2005 seasons, Teter continued to win or place in all of her competitions, including the Winter X Games, the Grand Prix, World Cup competitions, and the Vans Triple Crown. In 2005, Teter was ranked second among American halfpipe snowboarders. In first place was Gretchen Bleiler, a snowboarder and part-time model. Bleiler is five years older than Teter. Both competitors earned spots on the U.S. Olympic team to compete in the 2006 Winter Olympics in Turin, Italy. (For more information on Gretchen Bleiler, see *Biography Today Sports,* Vol. 13.)

Teter appeared with other top snowboarders in the movie First Descent.

First Descent

In 2005, filmmakers Kevin Harrison and Kemp Curley directed a film titled *First Descent: The Story of the Snowboarding Revolution.* As the name implies, the movie is all about the sport of snowboarding. The term "first descent" is actually a snowboarding expression. It is used to describe snowboarding down a mountain that no one else has been down before. The thrill of a first descent is that no one is sure what will happen if they snowboard down that mountain.

In this nonfiction film, famous snowboarders spend two weeks in Alaska doing what they do best—snowboarding. Between the snowboarding scenes, the movie features profiles of the participating snowboarders, including Teter and fellow 2006 Olympic gold medalist Shaun White. (For more information on Shaun White, see *Biography Today Sports,* Vol. 14.)

The 2006 Winter Olympics

Snowboarding was first introduced as an Olympic sport during the 1998 Winter Olympics in Nagano, Japan. At the time, snowboarding was growing in popularity, particularly among younger enthusiasts. By 2006, the National Sporting Goods Association estimated that the United States had more recreational snowboarders (6.6 million) than skiers (5.9 million).

During the 2006 Winter Olympics, the United States men's and women's teams dominated the snowboarding events. On February 12, Shaun White won the gold medal and Danny Kass won the silver medal for the United States. The women's competition was the next day, and Teter and Bleiler were to compete in the halfpipe.

Teter competing in the halfpipe finals at the 2006 Winter Olympics.

In the halfpipe competition, the snowboard competitors complete two runs, about an hour apart. Only the best run counts. After the first run, Teter was the leader. She did not need to go all out for the second run, but it wasn't her style to hold back. She did even better on the second run, making her the clear gold medal winner. Bleiler won the silver medal.

Before that second run, Teter and Bleiler, who have become good friends, decided to do a couple of practice runs to calm their nerves. The two snuck away and found an area with fresh snow. It turns out that it was a restricted area, but they couldn't resist. According to Teter, "We had about a half hour 'til finals and we went all the way up to the top of the mountain. It was good. We just kind of relaxed on the lifts and soaked up the sun and really just felt good." Bleiler added, "We didn't realize the entire mountain was blocked off. We had to cut under some ropes—sorry, but we did—and we found some powder. So we get some powder in, and we come down, and she got the gold medal and I got a silver medal. Voila. That's snowboarding."

It was always Teter's dream to compete in the Olympics, and her dream came true. With her family there to cheer her on, she gave her best performance and won the gold. Although Teter competed to win, she didn't focus on the outcome. "It's all about fun, because it's just a crazy path I get to lead right now," she said. "I'm focused on the inner self and getting along with everyone. It's about loving one another. It's not about beating people. It's about doing what you like to do."

U.S. snowboarding coach Bud Keene said of Teter, "Hannah has sparked a revolution. At 15, she was going bigger than anyone has ever gone. The others said, 'Whoa, who is this kid?'"

"

Teter competes to win, but she doesn't focus on the outcome. "It's all about fun, because it's just a crazy path I get to lead right now," she said. "I'm focused on the inner self and getting along with everyone. It's about loving one another. It's not about beating people. It's about doing what you like to do."

"

Life after the Olympics

When asked how winning a gold medal would affect her life, Teter said, "I don't think I'm going to change. Maybe I'll smile a little more. Get my teeth whitened. I might actually be able to buy a boat so I can go wakeboarding." Teter is expected to compete in the 2010 Olympics, too. After all the hard work she put into winning the gold medal, she said, "Now I just want to go to the beach and relax. I will see you in Hawaii."

Teter has not had much of a chance to relax. Since winning gold medals, she and White are the most sought after U.S. Olympians. Teter has received frequent requests to make guest appearances on television shows and at special events. For example, she made granola with Martha Stewart on TV; was a guest on the "Late Night with David Letterman" show; and she and Bleiler even got to wave the green flag to signal the start of the Daytona 500, a major stock car race held in Daytona, Florida.

Despite the hectic pace, Teter seemed to be enjoying herself. "It's gotten busier," she said, "Way busier. I've gotten to meet a whole bunch of people and travel to a whole bunch of places. It's been fun. It's been different." She continued, "I went to the Olympics thinking, 'This is cool; it's the biggest event in snowboarding.' Everybody from around the world gets to see you. Doing well, I didn't know the opportunities it brought in. I hadn't thought that far. This is all new and crazy."

"I'm just having fun. That's my main priority—just to keep having fun, keep everything positive. That's when I do my best—when I'm having a good time."

Having Fun

Despite all the publicity, Teter has remained level-headed. She said, "I'm just having fun. That's my main priority—just to keep having fun, keep everything positive. That's when I do my best—when I'm having a good time." According to Amen, Teter's oldest brother and manager, that's the essence of snowboarding. "It's having fun. It's going out with your friends and enjoying yourself. It's actually amazing you can go out and make a career out of it." It's a lifestyle that his sister is enjoying, according to Amen: "I'm definitely biased, but she is just this free-spirited young girl who doesn't have any qualms about saying, 'This is fun.'"

When asked about the key to her success, Teter replied, "There are a lot of combinations of things that have added up to bless me with this lifestyle. It doesn't come easy to be a pro snowboarder. It takes a lot of hard work, time, dedication, love, passion, support, and most of all, it takes failure and learning to better yourself from it."

Teter would like to be a role model for young kids, especially girls, who want to pursue snowboarding as a sport. "I just want to be a positive figure," she claimed. "My dream has always been to be the good role model and just put out good energy and motivation and inspiration for girls who are just like me." When asked what advice she would give to someone who wants to achieve a goal, she replied, "Focus your mindset, know what you want, love what you have, and give it all you've got!"

HOME AND FAMILY

Teter owns a home in South Lake Tahoe, California. Abe and Elijah live there with her, so she spends a lot of time with them. She also spends a lot of time with Amen, who is her manager. "It is the biggest blessing in the world to travel with three of my brothers," she said. "I couldn't ask for more. They help me out when I'm feeling stressed or overwhelmed with things. They cheer me on when I'm about to drop into the pipe in a contest. They just give me a strong sense of comfort so I'm always at peak performance levels." Teter also gets lots of love and support from her parents. She depends on all of them and often talks about "the fam thing."

Religion is a big part of Teter's life. The Teter family home in Vermont is near a Benedictine monastery, and Teter often goes there to meditate. She said, "I go there and kind of forget about everything—my life, my stresses, my world. They are soooo cool, they are soooo fun, and they're just super smart and jolly, you know?" Teter's parents wanted their children to make their own decisions about their faith. "We have our faith, but our mom let us all go in different directions and see what we figured out," Teter said. She described her own beliefs like this: "I'm focused on the inner self. The love—just the people of the world, and trying to get along with everyone. That's kind of what I figured out. It's about lovin' one another."

MAJOR INFLUENCES

Teter has credited her brothers with introducing her to snowboarding. She learned many of her moves by watching them and then came up with her own style. She said of her brothers, "They were my foundation. Then you grow in your own direction. You become your own tree."

Family is very important to Teter, and she talks about them all the time. "Family is the foundation of everything," she said. "This is a family thing. I got my no-fear attitude from my brothers from back when we used to bounce on the trampoline or go to the skate park."

"I just want to be a positive figure," Teter claimed. "My dream has always been to be the good role model and just put out good energy and motivation and inspiration for girls who are just like me."

HOBBIES AND OTHER INTERESTS

When Teter is not snowboarding, she likes to practice yoga. She also likes to skateboard, hoola hoop, jump off rope swings, and bounce on the trampoline. She used to play soccer, but she had to give that up when she started to focus on snowboarding.

The whole Teter family loves maple syrup. Teter always carries a lucky bottle of syrup with her when she competes. When the Teter kids were growing up, they would make their own syrup. "The family would go in the woods together and collect the sap out of the buckets we hung on the trees," Teter recalled. "Then we would bring it back to the sugar shack in our yard and hang out with my dad while he boiled it down. Once it was done, we'd get a bowl of snow and pour the syrup on it. It's a super-good treat. We still do it every year."

Teter loves syrup so much that she decided to use it as a way to help others. She is selling her family's syrup, which she named Hannah's Gold, to earn money for World Vision, a Christian relief organization that helps children and their communities. "I've always wanted to give back after receiving so much," she said. "Snowboarding has given me the opportunity to make this dream come true. This one-of-a kind Grade A Maple Syrup is being dedicated to the desperately poor children of Africa. Through my partnership with World Vision, this project will be helping those in greatest need."

MOVIES

First Descent: The Story of the Snowboarding Revolution, 2005

HONORS AND AWARDS

Competitor of the Year Award (North American Snowsports Journalist Association): 2004
World Snowboard Championship: 2004, Bronze Medal
Olympic Games, Halfpipe Snowboard: 2006, Gold Medal
ESPY Awards: 2006, for Best Women's Action Sports Athlete

FURTHER READING

Periodicals

Boston Globe, Mar. 16, 2006, p.C12
Boston Herald, Feb. 11, 2006, p.O47
Daily Variety, Dec. 2, 2005, p.6
Houston Chronicle, Feb. 14, 2006, p.1
San Francisco Chronicle, Feb. 9, 2006, p.O6
Sports Illustrated, Feb. 27, 2006, p.35
Sports Illustrated for Kids, Feb. 1, 2004, p.56
Time, Feb. 27, 2006, p.60
Time for Kids, Mar. 3, 2006, p.8
Your Magazine, Jan. 2004, p.12

ADDRESS

Hannah Teter
U.S. Ski and Snowboard Association
P.O. Box 100
1500 Kearns Blvd.
Park City, UT 84060-0100

WORLD WIDE WEB SITES

http://usolympicteam.com
http://www.ussnowboarding.com
http://www.vermontel.net/~teter

BRIEF ENTRY

Tyler James Williams 1992-

American Actor
Star of the Hit Television Show "Everybody Hates Chris"

EARLY YEARS

Tyler James Williams was born on October 9, 1992, in New York, New York. His father, Le'Roy Williams, is a sergeant for the New York City Police Department. His mother, Angela Williams, is a Christian singer, songwriter, and founder of Little Light Publishing Company. Tyler is the oldest of three boys. His younger brothers, Tyrel and Tylen, are also actors.

Williams has been acting practically his entire life. He began acting when he was only four years old. "I never decided to become an actor," he said. "It just came to me. I just performed for my mother, doing impersonations of people when I was little. People were impressed with what they saw me doing, and we contacted an agent and that was that."

Starting at age four, Williams began acting on "Sesame Street," the educational children's television show that has been on the air since 1969. "Sesame Street" uses short, fast-paced segments to teach preschool-aged children beginning number and reading skills. The show includes both people and muppets, the beloved puppets created by Jim Henson, including Big Bird, Cookie Monster, Elmo, and Kermit the Frog. Williams made regular appearances on "Sesame Street" between 1996 and 2002.

In 1999, Williams joined the cast of "Little Bill," an animated television series that aired on Nickelodeon. The show was created by comedian and actor Bill Cosby for preschool-aged children. Williams provided the voice for the character Bobby.

Williams appeared in several television commercials and print advertisements for such products as Fruit by the Foot (a chewy fruit snack) and Corvette (a high performance sports car). He also performed several times on NBC's popular late-night, comedy-variety show, "Saturday Night Live." His parts on "Saturday Night Live" were relatively small, so he spent a lot of time waiting on the set. But while he was waiting, he watched the other actors practicing their parts. "I got to watch them try and make scenes funnier, and how they worked on their timing," he confided. "That kind of helped me when I auditioned for 'Everybody Hates Chris.'"

"

"I never decided to become an actor," Williams said. "It just came to me. I just performed for my mother, doing impersonations of people when I was little. People were impressed with what they saw me doing, and we contacted an agent and that was that."

"

MAJOR ACCOMPLISHMENTS

Auditioning for a New Show

In 2005, comedian and actor Chris Rock and his business partner Ali LeRoi had an idea for a show. They wanted to create a comedy series that chronicled Rock's life as a black teenager attending a mostly white school. When

Williams appearing with comedian Chris Rock, co-creator and executive producer of "Everybody Hates Chris."

Rock was 13 years old, his family had moved from a housing project to an apartment in the Bedford-Stuyvesant neighborhood in Brooklyn, New York. Bed-Stuy, as it's known, is a predominantly African-American community. His parents wanted him to get a good education, and they decided to send Rock to a junior high school that was three bus routes away from their home.

Rock and LeRoi decided to call the show "Everybody Hates Chris" and held auditions in California. According to LeRoi, "We started looking for someone in L.A., and what we found was that we were encountering the usual suspects. They're Hollywood kids who have been in the business for a few years. We were looking for someone who was a little raw and a little edgier. And we got [an audition] tape from New York with this kid on it." The kid on that tape was Williams. Rock and LeRoi knew right away that Williams was the right person to play the main character. LeRoi said, "The thing that sold us was his face. He has an incredibly expressive face, and it's older than his years. . . . At this particular point, there's no Hollywood in him."

Williams flew to Los Angeles for two more auditions and was given the part. Rock and LeRoi were very pleased with his performances. According to Rock, "He was the funniest kid we could find after thousands of auditions. Let me tell you, after doing all those auditions, there are lots of unfunny kids out there who need to work on their comedy."

When Williams read the script for "Everybody Hates Chris," he thought it was a good fit for him. He felt that he connected with the character. One thing that he did not like about the script was that some of his lines included swear words and crude language. "I told them up front I wasn't going to say any of those words," he recalled. When he was reading his lines, Williams looked at how the word was used. "If it is appropriate, if it can help the character or help someone else, I'll use it," he said. "Or I try to come up with a word that is just as funny." His mom, Angela, was proud of her son. "Every time he went in and auditioned, he substituted the word," she commented. "We're Christians, and there are certain things we just don't do." Rock did not pressure Williams to use those words, but he did ask him to think about it. But Angela said that her son still did not curse. "He nailed the script," she said. "He did what he was supposed to do, but he stayed true to who he was. I was just really so proud of him."

"

"Kids like Tyler come around only once in a generation," Chris Rock said. "I thank God every day for this little kid being on our show because some kids have it, some kids don't. It's not about being a little adult; it's about being a kid portraying a kid, and I think that America gets it when he does it."

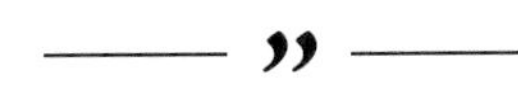

"Everybody Hates Chris"

"Everybody Hates Chris" debuted in September 2005 on UPN (now part of the new CW network). For the first episode, almost eight million viewers tuned in—the highest number of viewers for any show on UPN. Williams played the part of the young Chris Rock perfectly, and the show has continued to do well in the TV ratings.

Set in 1982, "Everybody Loves Chris" is narrated by Chris Rock. Williams's television father is played by former National Football League (NFL) player Terry Crews; his mother is played by actress Tichina Arnold. Like Rock's own parents, the parents on the show are loving and supportive, and they want the best for their children. Money is tight for the family, but they manage to make it work.

Williams's character faces many obstacles in school, as one of the few African-American students there. The show presents some of the difficul-

ties Rock faced in real life in a humorous light. As Rock later admitted, "I went through all this stuff. It wasn't funny at the time, but tragedy plus time equals comedy, as they say. I'm over it. Hey, I won. That's how I look at it."

"Everybody Hates Chris" does not focus only on Rock's school experiences. It is a family show, and much of the show is about his family life—his relationship with his parents and his siblings. Many have called it a refreshing look at life for a stable American family. "I just wanted to show a normal happy family," Rock explained. "There aren't a lot of poor people on TV, and it's kind of interesting to see a poor family trying to make it."

Rock is often on the set during filming of the show, and he has had great things to say about working with Williams. "Kids like Tyler come around only once in a generation. I thank God every day for this little kid being on our show because some kids have it, some kids don't. . . . It's not about being a little adult; it's about being a kid portraying a kid, and I think that America gets it when he does it."

Williams is equally eager to praise Rock. "It's fun working with him," he said. "He gives us jokes to come up with for the show, and we get to ad-lib sometimes." Williams respects Rock as an actor, comedian, and family man. He said that Rock is "an awesome comedian. He's also a husband and a daddy. One time we were doing an interview together and Chris stopped it because his little girl called. I think that was the best thing in the world."

Recent Activities

As "Everybody Hates Chris" grew in popularity, Williams began to get offers for other television shows and movies. He has made guest appearances on many popular talk shows, including "The Oprah Winfrey Show." He also had minor roles in two recent movies. He had a small part in *Two for the Money* (2005), an adult movie about sports, gambling, and crime. He had another small part, a voiceover role, in *The Ant Bully* (2006), an animated kids' movie about a boy who tortures some ants by destroying their colony with a watergun and then is reduced to their size. Even with his busy TV schedule, Williams would still consider additional movie roles, especially when "Everybody Hates Chris" has a break in its production schedule. "Offers are coming in, and there might be an acting job during the hiatus," he said.

Despite the popularity of his TV show, Williams has not let his success go to his head. He works hard to keep his priorities in line. His mother said that "Tyler totally gets it. He's extremely grounded. My husband and I made sure of that with all three of our kids. He's into learning and making that part of his life a priority. He also knows this show is a team effort—he isn't doing this show by himself."

———— " ————

Sometimes Williams misses New York. "I miss some of my friends, but other friends, I can do without 'em a little bit," he admitted. "Besides, I'm sort of too busy to really spend much time thinking about that part of my life."

———— " ————

Education

Williams's parents have always stressed the importance of education. However, because Williams spends so much of his time filming "Everybody Hates Chris," he does not attend a regular school. He and the other child actors on the show have a tutor on the set. They attend classes five days a week for three hours each of those days. His favorite subjects are science and history. His least favorite subject is English. He said, "Diagramming sentences gives me a headache."

According to American child-labor laws, children cannot work more than nine-and-a-half hours a day, and three of those hours must be spent doing school work. This makes it hard for the producers of "Everybody Hates Chris." They have to come up with creative ways to minimize each child's time in front of the camera. One way around this is to minimize the number of scenes in which all of them are together. That way they can stagger the filming time. However, since Williams is the main character and needs to be present in most of the scenes, it's a challenge. It's been difficult to limit his work time, but they have managed to work it out.

Williams with his parents, Le'Roy and Angela Williams, at the 2006 NAACP Image Awards.

HOME AND FAMILY

Williams lives with his parents, brothers, and their silky terrier named Benny "Ruff-neck" Williams. Their family home is in New York. But because "Everybody Hates Chris" is filmed in California, Williams, his brothers, and their mother spend most of their time in Los Angeles. Williams's father has stayed behind in New York because of his job. He has been with the New York Police Department for over 18 years. Williams admires his dad. "He's a sergeant, and he works out of a precinct. I'm pretty proud of him." The family flies back and forth a lot to spend time together.

Sometimes Williams misses New York. "I miss some of my friends, but other friends, I can do without 'em a little bit," he admitted. "Besides, I'm sort of too busy to really spend much time thinking about that part of my life."

HOBBIES AND OTHER INTERESTS

Williams loves to watch basketball. His favorite professional basketball team is the Miami Heat. He also used to like playing football. He said. "But I can't do that much anymore. It's in my contract—so I won't get hurt."

SELECTED CREDITS

Television Series

"Sesame Street," 1996-2002
"Little Bill," 1999
"Everybody Hates Chris," 2005-

Movies

Two for the Money, 2005
The Ant Bully, 2006

FURTHER READING

Books

Contemporary Theatre, Film, and Television, Vol. 68, 2006

Periodicals

Bergen County (NJ) Record, July 31, 2005, p.E1
Ebony, Jan. 2006, p.26; Mar. 2006, p.123
Jet, Oct. 10, 2005, p.60
Parade Magazine, Feb. 12, 2006, p.20
People, Oct, 17, 2005, p.134
TelevisionWeek, June 27, 2005, p.11

Online Articles

http://www.hollywoodreporter.com
(*TheHollywoodReporter.com,* "Laugh Track," Nov. 16, 2005)

Online Databases

Biography Resource Center Online, 2006, article from *Contemporary Theatre, Film, and Television,* 2006

ADDRESS

Tyler James Williams
CW Television Network
3300 W. Olive Ave.
Burbank, CA 91505

WORLD WIDE WEB SITES

http://tylerjameswilliams.com
http://www.cwtv.com

Gretchen Wilson 1973-

American Country Music Singer and Songwriter
Creator of the Hit CDs *Here for the Party* and *All Jacked Up*

BIRTH

Gretchen Wilson was born on June 26, 1973, in Granite City, Illinois. Her mother, Christine Heuer, was only 16 years old at the time of Gretchen's birth. Her father, who left the family when Gretchen was two years old, was a traveling musician. Divorced twice by age 20, Christine Heuer supported her family by working as a bartender. Gretchen has a younger brother, Josh, who sells souvenirs at her concerts.

YOUTH

Wilson spent most of her childhood constantly moving from one rented mobile home to another in rural Bond County, Illinois, about 40 miles east of St. Louis, Missouri. Her family crisscrossed the county's cornfields and pig farms, living in a string of trailer parks on the outskirts of numerous small towns. "We couldn't make the rent, so we'd move," Wilson explained. She mainly grew up in the area around Pocahontas, Illinois (population about 800), which she has described as "the kind of place where everybody knows everybody's business. It's the kind of place you can't get away with anything."

Wilson began singing at an early age. She performed regularly at family gatherings and even entertained shoppers at a local Kmart store. She has said that her singing talent comes from her father, whom she has not publicly named. "His family," she recalled, "had a little traveling band. I think it was a gospel band." Wilson has no early memories of her father, who left when she was two years old. She met him for the first time at age 12. "I think he felt he'd done the wrong thing," she has said of their time spent apart. "I think he felt my mom would do better without him, so he stepped back." Wilson has forgiven her father for his absence from her childhood, and the two are now friends. "I've been pretty understanding," she explained, "knowing they were both kids [when I was born]. I don't hold a grudge against him."

"I thought everybody was redneck when I was a kid," Wilson explained. "I thought everybody had a single mom who worked two jobs and had peanut butter and jelly three nights a week for supper."

Meanwhile, Wilson's mother, Christine Heuer, juggled bartending jobs and raised her two children alone. "I thought everybody was redneck when I was a kid," Wilson explained. "I thought everybody had a single mom who worked two jobs and had peanut butter and jelly three nights a week for supper." Because of her mother's busy schedule, Gretchen usually took care of her brother, Josh. Commenting on her relationship with her mother, Wilson remarked, "There was tension between me and my mom because we were so close in age. We were almost like sisters. By about 12, I felt like the grownup in the house."

In times of stress, Wilson drew comfort from listening to music. She recalled that as a young girl, "music sometimes felt like it was the only thing that kept me going when things got incredibly tough." She has expressed the hope that her music can help others, as the music of Patsy Cline and Loretta Lynn helped her as an adolescent. "When I was a kid, I'd sit there with my headphones on crying my eyes out to sad songs [I'd] taped off the radio. Somehow it made me feel better to know that someone else had the same kind of heartbreak I had," Wilson stated. "I remember listening to [Patsy Cline] when I was 12 and how she made me understand what heartache felt in a way I don't think many 12-year-olds can even begin to feel. She was the one who made me want to sing." George Jones and Merle Haggard were two other favorites, along with several hard rock bands, especially AC/DC and .38 Special.

EDUCATION

Because her family moved so often, Wilson attended about 20 different schools. She dropped out of school after the eighth grade and went to work with her mother in a bar. "When you're a kid, you think you know it all," she said. "I thought, 'Why do I need a high-school diploma?' I figured I was going to be a singer." She added, "Looking back, it was a stupid way to think." Wilson has expressed regret about dropping out of school and has talked about returning to school for a GED, a certificate of high school equivalency. Despite her lack of formal education, Wilson is considered an intelligent and skillful businesswoman. As her road manager David Haskell commented in the *Los Angeles Times,* "Gretchen may only have an eighth-grade education, but she's got a PhD in street smarts."

FIRST JOBS

At age 14, Wilson started working at a tavern known locally as "Big O's" in Pierron, five miles outside Pocahontas. She cooked while her mother tended bar. "This place was mostly friends and family—it was like daycare," Wilson remarked. "I don't think anybody thought I was in danger there. My mom was there, and everybody knew everybody. If anybody caused any trouble, we'd just call his wife and have him dragged out of there. It was always a big family of people."

The owner of the bar, Mark "Big O" Obermark, agreed to let Wilson sing for tips. She usually sang along to tape recordings of her favorite country singers, Loretta Lynn and Patsy Cline. She'd leave a jar out for the bar patrons to fill with tips. "I started out with nine songs, and I'd sing them over and over again all night. I was playing to happy-hour, middle-aged crowds, and they thought I was cute. Before it was over with, I was booking four nights a week for $125 a night."

Within a year, Wilson was promoted to bar manager, an illegal but not uncommon practice in rural areas. Since her new job sometimes required her to kick out unruly patrons, she had to be prepared, if necessary, to use the loaded, 12-gauge shotgun that hung in the bar. When she turned 16, she rented a microphone, amplifier, and tape player from a nearby music store and took her singing act to neighboring bars. Wilson performed karaoke-style at local bars while living with her uncle, Vernon "Verne" Heuer, who introduced her to the southern-rock groups Lynyrd Skynyrd and the Charlie Daniels Band. By the age of 20, Wilson was singing with two local bands, Sam A. Lama & the Ding Dongs, which covered songs of the "golden oldies" era, and Midnight Flyer, which often performed in suburban St. Louis. She also learned to play drums and electric, acoustic, and rhythm guitar. Wilson soon landed a gig fronting the rock-'n'-roll cover band Baywolfe, which became one of the busiest rock groups in the St. Louis region during the mid-1990s.

"

"I certainly think Nashville had this mold that everybody was supposed to fit into. . . . When I was getting a deal, everybody wanted [the women] to be Shania Twain and Faith Hill. And I definitely didn't fit into that mold."

"

CAREER HIGHLIGHTS

In 1996, Wilson moved to Nashville, Tennessee, the country music capital of the United States. She had $500 in her pocket and big hopes of signing a contract with a major recording company. For the next several years, she auditioned her singing talent for many recording executives, who politely rejected her for a variety of reasons. "They thought my hair was too dated, that I was too heavy, too old," she recalled. Others responded to her audition with the comment, "I'm sorry, but that's just too country," after which Wilson wondered, "How can you be too country for country?" As she later said, "I certainly think Nashville had this mold that everybody was supposed to fit into. . . . When I was getting a deal, everybody wanted [the women] to be Shania Twain and Faith Hill. And I definitely didn't fit into that mold."

In the meantime, Wilson found work as a cocktail waitress and bartender. She continued to work after she and her steady boyfriend, Mike Penner, had a baby daughter, Grace. With no record deal in sight, she considered putting aside her dream of a big singing career. "I always said if I didn't have a deal by 30, I would quit," she has claimed.

Wilson with Big Kenny and John Rich, who helped her get started in the music business in Nashville.

Connecting with MuzikMafia

In 1998, Wilson began singing on a regular basis with the house band at a blues club where she was working. During one of her performances the following year, Wilson impressed John Rich and "Big" Kenny Alphin, better known now as the duo Big & Rich. According to one account, Rich asked Big Kenny, "Was that as good as I thought it was? Did I just hear that?" "I think so," his friend replied. After she finished singing, Rich tried to talk to her, but she thought he was just looking for a date. "John followed me up to my little cubby hole upstairs with his trench coat and cowboy hat, and I think his exact words were, 'Hey, how come you ain't got a record deal yet?'" Wilson wasn't overwhelmed. "I looked at him in disgust [and] threw him a business card and a little homemade demo and said, 'I'm busy. I'm working right now.'"

Rich began telephoning Wilson repeatedly, but she didn't trust him, and she refused to return his calls. She eventually changed her mind and accepted his offer to join the MuzikMafia network, an informal group of musicians, singers, songwriters, and artists who showcased their talents in a Nashville bar each week. These artists rejected the cookie-cutter approach to musical talent so prevalent in Nashville's recording industry. Rich introduced Wilson to his friends in the local songwriting community, who helped her polish her style and develop some experience. Through these contacts, she began recording "demo" tapes—recordings of other songwriters' music and lyrics that are used to sell a song to a particular performer. She finally had enough material to audition in what's called a "showcase" for the record company e®©tives.

But Rich also encouraged Wilson to try writing her own songs. One night, they were watching country music videos featuring glamorous female singers. Wilson told Rich how much she disliked their diva image, declaring "I guess I'm a redneck woman." Her comment inspired him to jot down some lyrics. In less than an hour, Rich and Wilson wrote what would become her hit single "Redneck Woman."

In 2003, Wilson auditioned "Redneck Woman" for John Grady, the new president of Sony Music Nashville. Before she performed the song, according to Wilson, "[I decided] not to be who they wanted me to be, but to be who I am, like it or not. Before, I was trying to be polite. I was trying to sing songs I thought they'd like, and I was a little concerned about that. But it comes down to confidence, who you are as an artist." Grady immediately sensed the song's hit potential and signed Wilson to a recording contract. He was equally impressed by her stage presence, acknowledging that "it was the first time I was physically [moved] by a singer in a long time." Sony decided to release "Redneck Woman" as a single in early spring 2004. To express their pride in Wilson, the MuzikMafia named her the first Godmother of the Mafia in 2005.

"Redneck Woman"

With the release of "Redneck Woman," Wilson became the music success story of 2004. Anchored by its "Hell, yeah" refrain, the song became a rallying cry for the "redneck" way of life. "Redneck" has often been used as an insult to describe poor, ignorant country people. But Wilson turned that around and used it in a positive way. "To me, being a redneck woman means being a strong woman," she said. "It's about holding your head up no matter what is happening. I know the term used to have other meanings, but to me it's just another way of saying country." Her lyrics celebrated living an ordinary life, shopping for sale items at Wal-Mart and drinking beer instead of champagne: "I'm a redneck woman / I ain't no high class broad / I'm just a product of my raising / I say hey y'all and yee-haw / And I keep my Christmas lights on / On my front porch all year long / And I know all the words to every Charlie Daniels song."

Wilson's song also started a musical movement in Nashville by mixing traditional country music with elements of hard rock and hip-hop. "She has revitalized Nashville," declared Grady, president of Sony Music. Jon Bream of the Minneapolis *Star Tribune* wrote, "Wilson offers an uncompromising blend of Skynyrd, Strait, and cojones that will rock you like NASCAR, but comfort you like Oprah." Marc Oswald, one of Wilson's managers, commented on another unique aspect of her style: "She reminded everyone that they should be in the music business, not the image business. It has woken a lot of people up." Industry executives and reviewers alike have attested to her unique connection with her audience. Wilson seemed "closer to the audience than any performing musician out there today," said Grady. "She has no problem relating, and they have no problem identifying back with her. It's about empowerment."

> *"To me, being a redneck woman means being a strong woman," Wilson said. "It's about holding your head up no matter what is happening. I know the term used to have other meanings, but to me it's just another way of saying country."*

"Redneck Woman" was released as a single in April 2004. When the song rose to No. 1 in May, Wilson became the first solo female singer to top the *Billboard* Hot Country Songs chart in over two years. She also had the fastest-rising debut single on country music charts since LeAnn Rimes released "Blue" in 1996. Fans clearly responded to the authenticity of "Redneck Woman," which reflected Wilson's hard-living background and her personal philosophy of "being honest and true to yourself." "I talk all the time about my idols being Loretta Lynn and Tanya Tucker and Patsy Cline and people like that. And I knew when I listened to a Loretta Lynn record that I was going to hear stories that were real. I hung on every word that came out of her mouth because I knew that she had lived that."

Here for the Party

Wilson's first album, *Here for the Party,* was originally scheduled for release in July 2004, but the success of "Redneck Woman" caused Sony to push the date forward to May 2004. The album debuted at No. 2 on the *Billboard* 200 pop chart and No. 1 on the *Billboard* Top Country Albums chart, where it remained for nine consecutive weeks. It sold 227,000 copies in its opening week, breaking the sales record for a country music

album. *Here for the Party* became the bestselling country album of the year and the fifth bestselling album overall for 2004 with just under three million copies sold by year's end. These sales figures made Wilson the top-selling debut artist of any genre in 2004. Meanwhile, videos from *Here for the Party* appeared regularly on Country Music Television (CMT), most notably "When I Think about Cheatin'" and "Redneck Woman." The latter video features cameo appearances by Tanya Tucker, Big & Rich, Kid Rock, and Hank Williams Jr.

Here for the Party became an instant hit with audiences and critics. One explanation for the record's popularity was offered by radio executive Jessie Scott in an interview on National Public Radio. "Gretchen Wilson is maybe single-handedly bringing some soul back to country," Scott said. "And the reason why I say that is so much of what's come down over the course of the last several years has been so pop that it's soulless and it's homogenized. And this is fresh and free and wonderful, and, you know, the message is great, too."

Wilson's phenomenal breakthrough continued into the summer and fall of 2004. A hit at dance clubs, the single "Here for the Party" nearly matched the success of "Redneck Woman" on both the pop and country charts. Wilson also began touring at major arenas around the country. She opened for the Brooks & Dunn and Montgomery Gentry tour in the summer of 2004. By August, Wilson began to notice big changes in her life. "I have probably made and spent a quarter of a million dollars in the last four months," she marveled. "That's more money than I could ever think about four months ago. All of a sudden, I have a corporation. I have people that work for me that I don't even know."

The music industry and country music fans showered Wilson with recognition at annual award ceremonies. In 2004, she won the Country Music Association's Horizon Award, which is given to the top new artist of the year; she also won an American Music Award for best new artist. In 2005, she won a Grammy Award for best female country vocal performance on "Redneck Woman." During this show, Wilson participated in a special tribute performance of Lynryd Skynryd's rock anthem "Free Bird" with Tim McGraw, Keith Urban, and current Lynryd Skynryd singer Johnny Van Zant. She also won two awards for best videos at the 2005 Country Music Television Awards.

All Jacked Up

With her phenomenal rise to fame behind her, Wilson turned her attention to her next album. "Fans obviously loved her 'what you see is what you get' approach to the debut project, so it only makes sense to give them more of what they want," advised Jon Anthony, program director of XM Satellite Radio's country music station. Wilson began working on her second album, although some industry experts cautioned that it was too soon for a follow-up record. According to Grady, the second album "is more about her. . . . The first record defined her but from songwriting to song selection to musician selecting to producing to sequencing, she has played a far larger role in this one." During the summer of 2005, Wilson was the opening act on Kenny Chesney's "A Place in the Sun" tour, during which she performed several songs from her then-unreleased second album.

Wilson released her second album, *All Jacked Up*, in September 2005. The record debuted at No. 1 on both the *Billboard* 200 and Top Country Albums charts, selling more than 264,000 copies during its first week. Wilson reinforced her rough-edged image with such songs as "Politically Uncorrect,"

"One Bud Wiser," "Skoal Ring," and "All Jacked Up," but she also included songs written by other artists to show another side of her talent. She performed the new ballad "I Don't Feel Like Loving You Today," written by Matraca Berg and Jim Collins, which she has cited as her favorite song on the album. She also included a hidden track, a cover of the Billie Holiday song "Good Morning, Heartache," which many critics considered an exciting demonstration of the range of her talent.

All Jacked Up was a more modest success than Wilson's debut album. Still, she was recognized with several awards at the annual awards ceremonies. In 2005, she won the Country Music Association Award for female vocalist of the year and the American Music Award for favorite female country artist. She also earned nominations for the 2006 Grammy Awards, the Country Music Televisions Awards, and the Academy of Country Music Awards, but she lost to the competition on all counts.

CONTROVERSY AND BACKLASH

Despite her popularity among fans and industry professionals, Wilson's candid subject matter, explicit song lyrics, and tough-woman persona have met with criticism. In 2005, her song "Skoal Ring" became controversial. Skoal is a brand of chewing tobacco, and a Skoal ring is a round mark left in the back pocket of those who regularly carry a can of snuff in their jeans pocket. In concert, Wilson began holding up a can of Skoal because many fans thought the song referred to a "skull ring." These performances drew notice from Tennessee's attorney general, who objected to what he called the "promotion of smokeless products, particularly as it related to the youth who attend [her] concerts and listen to [her] music." He asked her to "avoid glamorizing and normalizing the use of smokeless tobacco products" by discontinuing her practice of raising a can of Skoal smokeless tobacco during her concerts. Wilson complied with the attorney general's request. "I don't want kids out there to go buy Skoal and start dipping because Gretchen Wilson does it," she maintained. "I'm a mother, and I wouldn't push tobacco or alcohol at a child." She does chew tobacco, or "dip," a habit she started as a way to help her stop smoking cigarettes. "I traded one evil for another," she confessed. "To be honest, I've realized now that quitting smoking was easier than quitting dipping. But I will eventually be free of nicotine. I know it."

"

"I'm just a simple, ordinary woman. I think that's a lot of the reason why people have really connected with me. I am just like them."

The lyrics of other songs have also been considered objectionable by some listeners, to which Wilson has consistently responded, "I don't apologize for the lyrics." She has often cited Loretta Lynn as a major influence on her career because "she spoke her mind, which isn't as common as you might think in the music business. Loretta put things into songs that no woman had ever said at that time." Wilson has said that success has not changed her. During a 2006 interview with "60 Minutes" correspondent Ed Bradley, she remarked, "I'm just a simple, ordinary woman. I think that's a lot of the reason why people have really connected with me. I am just like them."

Despite such controversy, Wilson has continued to impress her fans. In 2006, She was the headline act for the "Redneck Revolution" tour, traveling with Johnny and Donnie VanZant, formerly of Lynyrd Skynyrd and .38 Special, and Blaine Larsen. She described being the headline act on a tour

Wilson performing onstage in New York City, 2005.

as "a whole lot more pressure, a whole lot more excitement. You get all the stage, you get all the drama, you get to step on stage every night knowing that those people came to see you and not the act after you." Commenting on the high energy level of her concerts, she said, "My show is a little more like a rock show, probably, compared to other females in country music. I've got pyro and an incredible AC/DC light show going on, and we're blowing stuff up, and it's loud and crazy and it's definitely rock 'n' roll." As for her fans, Wilson said, "They're unbelievable. They're on their feet from the moment the intro tape starts until the curtain comes down, and they sing along with every word to songs that haven't even been released. It's amazing."

HOME AND FAMILY

Shortly after she arrived in Nashville, Wilson began a relationship with Mike Penner, a nightclub owner. In 2001 they had a daughter, Grace. The couple never married and parted ways in 2005. Wilson makes her home with her daughter, Grace, and her mother, Christine Heuer. They live in a 4,000-square-foot house on a 17-acre estate outside Nashville, complete with a six-stall barn and nine animals.

HOBBIES AND OTHER INTERESTS

Wilson's hobbies include fishing, driving a four-wheeler, and spending time with her daughter. She has also expressed an interest in charitable activities. For example, on September 10, 2005, she performed at the Mississippi Coliseum in Jackson, Mississippi, as part of a concert to benefit victims of Hurricane Katrina. MTV, VH1, and CMT broadcast the Hurricane Katrina Relief concert, and proceeds were donated to CMT's "One Country," a new campaign that raises money for natural disaster relief. Money from this fund is disbursed among the American Red Cross, America's Second Harvest, Habitat for Humanity, the USA Boys & Girls Clubs, and Hands on America.

RECORDINGS

Here for the Party, 2004
All Jacked Up, 2005
Gretchen Wilson: Undressed (DVD), 2006

HONORS AND AWARDS

Horizon Award (Country Music Association): 2004
American Music Award: 2004, Favorite Breakthrough New Artist; 2005, Favorite Female Country Artist
Grammy Award (The Recording Academy): 2005, Best Female Country Vocal Performance, for "Redneck Woman"
Country Music Television Awards: 2005 (two awards), Best Breakthrough Video for "Redneck Woman" and Best Female Video for "When I Think about Cheatin'"
Academy of Country Music Awards: 2005 (two awards), Top Female Vocalist and Top New Artist
Country Music Association Award: 2005, Female Vocalist of the Year

FURTHER READING

Books

Contemporary Musicians, Vol. 52, 2005

Periodicals

Billboard, Sep. 24, 2005, p.50
Boston Globe, May 30, 2004, p.N1
Chicago Tribune, May 7, 2004, Tempo section, p.1
Entertainment Weekly, May 14, 2004, p.38; Oct. 29, 2004, p.14; Apr. 22, 2005, p.20
Los Angeles Times, Jan. 22, 2006, p.E1
New York Times, May 30, 2004, section 2, p.25
St. Louis Post-Dispatch, May 9, 2004, p.F1; May 27, 2004, p.23; Sep. 25, 2005, p.F1
USA Today, June 17, 2004, p.D1; Sep. 28, 2005, p.D6

Online Articles

http://www.allmusic.com
(All Music Guide, "Gretchen Wilson," undated)
http://www.npr.org
(National Public Radio, All Things Considered, "'Redneck Woman' Rules Country Charts," May 31, 2004)

Online Databases

Biography Resource Center Online, 2006, article from *Contemporary Musicians,* 2005

ADDRESS

Gretchen Wilson
Sony Music Nashville
1400 18th Ave., South
Nashville, TN 37212

WORLD WIDE WEB SITES

http://www.gretchenwilson.com
http://www.gretchenontour.com
http://www.muzikmafia.com

Photo and Illustration Credits

Bono/Photos: NewsCom.com (p. 9); Tim Mosenfelder/ImageDirect/Getty Images (p. 13); Anton Corbijn/copyright © 2006 Universal Music Group (p. 21); AP Images (p. 23). CD covers: HOW TO DISMANTLE AN ATOMIC BOMB (Interscope) copyright © 2006 Universal Music Group; THE JOSHUA TREE (Island) copyright © 2006 Universal Music; WAR (Island) copyright © 2006 Universal Music Group. Front cover: Jo Hale/ Getty Images.

Kelsie Buckley/Photos: AP Images (pp. 30, 33, 35).

Cynthia Kadohata/Photos: AP Images (p. 38); George Miyamoto (p. 42). Covers: KIRA-KIRA (Atheneum/Simon & Schuster) copyright © 2004 by Cynthia Kadohata. Jacket photograph copyright © 2004 by Julia Kuskin; WEEDFLOWER (Atheneum/Simon & Schuster) copyright © 2006 by Cynthia Kadohata. Jacket photographs and photo-illustration copyright © 2006 by Kamil Vojnar.

Coretta Scott King/Photos: NewsCom.com (p. 50); John Vacha/FPG/Getty Images (p. 52); AP Images (pp. 55, 58, 61, 66, front cover); courtesy Ronald Reagan Library (p. 65). Cover: MY LIFE WITH MARTIN LUTHER KING, JR. (Henry Holt and Company) copyright © 1969 by Coretta Scott King. Revised edition copyright © 1993 by Coretta Scott King.

Cesar Millan/Photos: copyright © National Geographic Channel (pp. 73, 76, 79); Nicholas Ellingsworth/copyright © MPH Entertainment (p. 80). Cover: CESAR'S WAY (Harmony/Crown) copyright © 2006 by Cesar Millan and Melissa Jo Peltier. Jacket copyright © 2006 by Harmony Books.

Nick Park/Photos: courtesy DreamWorks Distribution LLC (pp. 84, 88); copyright © Richard Keith Wolff/Retna (p. 90); AP Images (p. 92); courtesy of DreamWorks Pictures (p. 94, front cover); courtesy DreamWorks Animation SKG. Copyright © and TM Aardman Animations Ltd. (p. 97).

Ben Roethlisberger/Photos: AP Images (pp. 102, 105, 107, 113); Grant Halverson/Getty Images (p. 109). Front cover: David Drapkin/Getty Images.

Jamie Lynn Spears/Photos: Andrew Macpherson/Nickelodeon (p. 118); AP Images (p. 120). Book/DVD/CD covers: ZOEY 101 BEACH PARTY (Scholastic) copyright © 2006 Apollo Media; ZOEY 101 SPRING BREAK-UP copyright © 2006 Apollo Media; ZOEY 101 MUSIC MIX (p) and copyright © 2006 Apollo Media.

Hannah Teter/Photos: USOC (p. 126); Jed Jacobsohn/Getty Images (p. 129); Joe Klamar/ AFP/Getty Images (p. 132); AP Images (p. 135). DVD cover: FIRST DESCENT copyright © 2005 Universal Studios/copyright © 2005 Pepsi-Cola Advertising and Marketing.

Tyler James Williams/Photos: The CW (p. 138); Frederick M. Brown/Getty Images (pp. 140, 144); NewsCom.com (p. 142).

Gretchen Wilson/Photos: Kristin Barlowe (p. 146); Kevin Parry/WireImage.com (p. 150); Paul Hawthorne/Getty Images (p. 157). DVD covers: ALL JACKED UP (Epic) copyright © 2006 Sony Music Entertainment Inc.; HERE FOR THE PARTY (Epic) copyright © 2006 Sony Music Entertainment Inc.

Cumulative Names Index

This cumulative index includes the names of all individuals profiled in *Biography Today* since the debut of the series in 1992.

For cumulative general, places of birth, and birthday indexes, please see biographytoday.com.

 For cumulative general, places of birth, and birthday indexes, please see biographytoday.com.

 For cumulative general, places of birth, and birthday indexes, please see biographytoday.com.

For cumulative general, places of birth, and birthday indexes, please see biographytoday.com.

 For cumulative general, places of birth, and birthday indexes, please see biographytoday.com.

For cumulative general, places of birth, and birthday indexes, please see biographytoday.com.

Biography Today

General Series

"*Biography Today* will be useful in elementary and middle school libraries and in public library children's collections where there is a need for biographies of current personalities. High schools serving reluctant readers may also want to consider a subscription."
— *Booklist,* American Library Association

"Highly recommended for the young adult audience. Readers will delight in the accessible, energetic, tell-all style; teachers, librarians, and parents will welcome the clever format [and] intelligent and informative text. It should prove especially useful in motivating 'reluctant' readers or literate nonreaders."
— *MultiCultural Review*

"Written in a friendly, almost chatty tone, the profiles offer quick, objective information. While coverage of current figures makes *Biography Today* a useful reference tool, an appealing format and wide scope make it a fun resource to browse." — *School Library Journal*

"The best source for current information at a level kids can understand."
— Kelly Bryant, School Librarian, Carlton, OR

"Easy for kids to read. We love it! Don't want to be without it."
— Lynn McWhirter, School Librarian, Rockford, IL

Biography Today **General Series** includes a unique combination of current biographical profiles that teachers and librarians — and the readers themselves — tell us are most appealing. The **General Series** is available as a 3-issue subscription; hardcover annual cumulation; or subscription plus cumulation.

Within the **General Series**, your readers will find a variety of sketches about:

- Authors
- Musicians
- Political leaders
- Sports figures
- Movie actresses & actors
- Cartoonists
- Scientists
- Astronauts
- TV personalities
- and the movers & shakers in many other fields!

ONE-YEAR SUBSCRIPTION

- 3 softcover issues, 6" x 9"
- Published in January, April, and September
- 1-year subscription, list price $62. **School and library price $60**
- 150 pages per issue
- 10 profiles per issue
- Contact sources for additional information
- Cumulative Names Index

HARDBOUND ANNUAL CUMULATION

- Sturdy 6" x 9" hardbound volume
- Published in December
- List price $69. **School and library price $62 per volume**
- 450 pages per volume
- 30 profiles — includes all profiles found in softcover issues for that calendar year
- Cumulative General Index

SUBSCRIPTION AND CUMULATION COMBINATION

- $99 for 3 softcover issues plus the hardbound volume

For Cumulative General, Places of Birth, and Birthday Indexes, please see www.biographytoday.com.